Successful Study

Successful Study is an essential guide for students embarking upon an education-related Foundation Degree without previous study experience.

The world of study at university can be a daunting and bewildering place for new students unfamiliar with academic processes such as writing essays and presenting portfolios. This book offers clear and straightforward explanations of how to prepare for study, how to work at higher education level and how to tackle assignments.

Covering all aspects of educational study, and based on the experiences of real education professionals, this new edition has been fully updated to include:

- clear links to work-based practices throughout
- advice for students with disabilities
- guidance on using e-resources
- tips for managing your learning and increasing motivation
- how to think critically
- reflective practice.

With case studies, tasks and opportunities for reflection, this accessible book has been specifically designed for those on Teaching Assistant, Early Years or related Foundation Degrees and will be an essential resource for those wanting to find the answers to study questions quickly and easily.

Christine Ritchie has worked in education for over 40 years, first as a teacher and then in further education since 2000. She has been a Programme Director for Foundation Degrees and so has direct experience of working with mature students in their first encounters with higher education.

Paul Thomas has worked with students in higher education as a study tutor for a number of years. The experience gained working one-to-one has enabled Paul to identify the difficulties students face when encountering academic study for the first time.

Successful Study

Skills for teaching assistants and early years practitioners

Second Edition

Christine Ritchie and Paul Thomas

LONDON AND NEW YORK

Second edition published 2014
by Routledge
2 Park Square, Milton Park, Abingdon, Oxon OX14 4RN

and by Routledge
711 Third Avenue, New York, NY 10017

Routledge is an imprint of the Taylor & Francis Group, an informa business

First edition published by David Fulton Publishers Ltd 2004

British Library Cataloguing in Publication Data
A catalogue record for this book is available from the British Library

Library of Congress Cataloging-in-Publication Data
Ritchie, Christine.
Successful study : skills for teaching assistants and early years practitioners / Christine Ritchie, Paul Thomas.– Second edition.
pages cm
1. Study skills–Handbooks, manuals, etc. 2. Teachers' assistants–Training of. 3. Education, Preschool–Handbooks, manuals, etc. I. Thomas, Paul. II. Title.
LB2395.R58 2014
371.30281–dc23 2013026374

ISBN: 978–0–415–70908–8 (hbk)
ISBN: 978–0–415–70909–5 (pbk)
ISBN: 978–1–315–06511–3 (ebk)

Typeset in Melior
by Keystroke, Station Road, Codsall, Wolverhampton

Printed and bound in Great Britain by
TJ International Ltd, Padstow, Cornwall

Contents

Acknowledgements

The authors wish to thank Canterbury Christ Church University Study Support Unit for the initial inspiration to write this book and for permission to adapt material. We would also like to thank Claire Alfrey, along with the tutors and students on the Foundation Degree programmes, for their encouragement, testing of resources and helpful, constructive comments. Thanks also to Anita Cooper and Bridget Somers for their contributions to the new edition.

Finally, thanks must go to our patient, supportive and loving families.

Introduction: what to expect at higher levels of study

Aim of this book

This book is aimed at supporting mature (aged 21 or over!) students as they enrol on Foundation Degrees and similar Higher Education (HE) programmes. Such programmes have been developed for those working with children and young people (e.g. in Schools, in Early Years settings or as Child Minders) and provide a study route towards academic qualifications whilst continuing to work. As such, the students are likely to embark upon their chosen academic programme of study with a wealth of workplace experience, a degree of confidence about their abilities in working with children, but possibly with some anxiety about entering HE study.

Anxiety may be caused by the many questions that run through the mind when considering a new course of study. These may include rather daunting questions such as 'Will I be clever enough?', 'How much time will I have to spend studying?', 'Who will look after the children?' and 'How will I begin to write an essay?' For most mature students, especially those facing study for the first time since leaving school, such questions raise frightening spectres of possible failure. However, they can also create a sense of excitement and determination to succeed. Although such groups of people may not consider themselves to be clever academically, they may have a desire to build upon their experiential learning in the workplace in order to gain a more thorough theoretical understanding and new qualifications. As a result of workplace reforms and ideas of life-long learning, opportunities for study are more readily available than ever before, from joining a school INSET training day to studying for a degree at university or college on a part-time basis. Information in this book has been written to help this group of students to prepare for academic work and to guide them through their course of study.

Accompanying such opportunities may be the apprehension associated with returning to study, after perhaps a considerable time lag, linked to feelings of not knowing what to expect during study and lack of confidence in one's academic abilities. This book will help to demystify academic practices for this group of professionals. In order to succeed academically, a student must know how to do something and how to do it well. Expectations of work and study at HE level are discussed so as to enable students to become more aware of the skills they need to develop in order to meet the expectations, thereby helping them to gain more confidence in their own ability to succeed.

How to use the book

Each chapter, broken down into subsections, offers advice surrounding one particular facet of study. Subsequent chapters build upon these facets. The aim is not to be prescriptive, but to outline the basic purposes and procedures behind each aspect of study. You can select the ideas and methods that suit your own needs, matched to development within your chosen course of study. It is not intended that the book be read from cover to cover – it has been written as a 'dip-in' book. Browse through it first to familiarise yourself with its content, and then use it as a reference book to help you to tackle different academic tasks as and when required.

Everyone has a different way of learning and will develop different study habits. You may know your own learning patterns already, such as whether you enjoy working with background music or in a silent environment, whether you learn from reading a book or prefer to listen to someone talking. HE institutions have also developed their own unique ways of working that have evolved over time. Therefore, although this book offers a generic view of study and ways of approaching assessment procedures, there may be slight variations in the requirements between different HE institutions. Combine information contained in this book with details of recommendations given by your course, and take these into account when making academic choices.

Many thoughts may have entered your mind when you sent off the application form to begin your new programme of study. Along with the anticipation of future success, perhaps there was also a feeling of having to 'do things the right way'. Although this book suggests the correct way to approach many different academic tasks, what may be right for one person or institution may not be right for another. Do not be put off by ideas or suggestions that you do not immediately understand, but take time to absorb new information and adjust to the expectations of study. Once you have absorbed the rules, you can relax and concentrate on working in an original and creative way. Do not be too afraid to ask questions or make mistakes – utilise the expertise of others and learn from any mistakes that you may make.

Further reading

At the end of each chapter there are suggestions to help you search for further reading: although these are not comprehensive, they may help you to locate reading material with similar themes. Books and websites, in particular, quickly go out of date or disappear as new resources become available. Titles and full details of online resources have therefore been kept to a minimum. Chapter 9, however, does offer more a more detailed list of further reading resources.

Finally, remember that you are in control. You chose the course of study, so it is your responsibility to make the most of the opportunities that you have selected for yourself. Whether or not you start reading this book with previous study experience, have confidence in your own ability to succeed in your chosen field!

1 Starting study: getting organised

Introduction

Whether you are thinking about engaging in study or have just signed on for a course, you will have questions to ask about the expectations of HE and may want to prepare so that you can make the most of the opportunities available to you. Beginning new study can be an exciting time, full of stimulating, challenging and enjoyable experiences that will help you to move forward in new directions. You will be expecting to gain knowledge and qualifications to enhance your working practice and your career. In doing so, you will probably discover more about yourself as a learner too!

This first chapter deals with some of the issues about which you may have questions as you start your studies. It is divided into two parts. Part 1 suggests ways in which you can prepare for independent study and Part 2 looks briefly at ways in which you can use your skills during taught sessions. Some links between these skills and assessment processes are also made.

Part 1: starting with you!

Learning should be active, i.e. something that actively involves you and to which you actively contribute. Understandably, some people have a preconceived idea that going to university or college is about listening to lectures and trying to absorb information – historically, this is how academia has been portrayed. However, academic work is not only about gaining new knowledge and writing essays; it is also about personal growth, gaining confidence and opening doors to new opportunities. The most important part in the learning process is the learner, i.e. you; – your interests and previous experiences, your enthusiasm and curiosity for your chosen field of study will be your most important assets. As a mature student entering higher education, you already possess a considerable amount of experience. This may be categorised under the headings of knowledge, skill and understanding:

- knowledge: what you know and have learned about your work through experience
- skill: how well you can do things
- understanding: an awareness of interrelationships.

Consider, for example, the knowledge, skill and understanding you already have from your workplace experiences by responding 'yes' or 'no' to the statements on page 3.

Your answers are more likely to be positive than negative. Each statement could be extended by giving specific details of tasks linked to the knowledge, skill and understanding that are required by your present workplace. All of these experiences you may take for granted, or dismiss as being unimportant, but all will help you with your studies. Study, in common with other types of work and experience, involves building up a store of knowledge, skill and understanding. It is therefore simply an extension of what you can already do, through learning new skills and rules, methods, procedures, approaches and boundaries: all of these can be improved with practice.

Embarking upon a new course of study, particularly in an unfamiliar environment, may bring about feelings of insecurity and make you doubt your ability to be successful. You may feel 'de-skilled' and out of your depth and this can initially be a real barrier to learning. However, if you remind yourself of the skills and successes that you have already acquired, then you are more likely to gain confidence quickly. Remember that 'new' experiences quickly become 'old' experiences and therefore become comfortable and familiar. As a mature student, you have much to give and gain from new study, so plan to adapt previous experiences to solve new problems.

Students with a disability

Students with a disability may face additional challenges when engaging in study, but with planning and preparation the barriers can be overcome. Legally, the Equality Act introduced in 2011 makes it unlawful for universities or colleges to treat disabled students less favourably because of their disability. The law makes it clear that 'reasonable adjustments' must be made to ensure that such students are not put at a substantial disadvantage. The disability coordinator or advisor at your institution will be in the best position to give information on the support and services available to meet your individual needs. Letting the institution know of any disability in advance of your arrival will help it to provide the right level of support from the beginning of your studies. Do not be afraid to be clear about your needs or to ask questions.

Knowledge, skill and understanding gained through work experiences

Statement	Yes	No
I understand the requirements of my current job and am efficient and effective in that role.		
I work well with other adults in the workplace, and contribute ideas that help towards ensuring the smooth running of the curriculum/environment.		
I am a good communicator – I listen well to others, and am able to explain tasks and ideas to children and adults.		
I understand the needs of the children/young people I work with, and have built up good working relationships with them.		
I am a skilled negotiator with children, helping to solve disputes and giving the children skills to solve their own problems.		
I keep clear, accurate records when required, and regularly share knowledge with other appropriate members of staff.		
I support the learning needs of children, and understand the demands of the curriculum in the areas in which I work.		
I consider myself as a member of the school team, and support other colleagues willingly through sharing working practices.		
I use my initiative to solve home and workplace problems, and often plan ahead to ensure successful outcomes.		
I am punctual, and able to work to deadlines and keep to set timetables.		
When I am tackling a new task or responsibility, I am not afraid to ask for help, and to learn from the experiences of others.		
I am confident in the workplace, and enjoy the challenges and variety offered to me during the working year.		
I am curious, and like to ask questions or find out more about new ideas.		
I am determined and persistent in my work, and like to see a task through to the end, working to my best ability.		
I am flexible in my approach to others and to setting tasks, and show understanding of the needs of others in my daily interactions.		

Using existing skills for study

Existing skill	Adapted for study
Communicating information to others in the classroom.	Engaging in discussion with tutor and other students.
Writing reports and plans for individual children.	Planning work for assignments.
Working as a member of a team.	Collaborating with other students to complete a task or project.
Engaging in INSET training or school workshop.	Learning through listening to lectures and in discussion.
Negotiating time, solving problems, balancing the budget at home.	Designing timetables, solving learning problems, balancing expenses.

Dyslexia

Some students experience difficulties during study and come to the realisation that dyslexia or Irlen's Syndrome is the cause of their problems. Dyslexia is a common learning difficulty that affects reading, spelling and short-term memory. This may mean that the effort of reading an academic text results in nothing being taken in! Mature students returning to study sometimes discover that a previously undiagnosed condition of dyslexia may explain educational problems that they experienced as a child as well as the difficulties they face as a new student. The disability advisor will be able to offer advice about obtaining a diagnosis and have information about support structures that will help in your studies. The support is likely to come in two ways; firstly, giving consideration when marking work, e.g. allowing additional time or discounting spelling errors, and secondly, offering strategies to support study, e.g. online or face-to-face tutorials. Tutors will also be able to offer support during lecture time, so do discuss your needs with them.

The study strategies outlined in this book will be helpful to all students, including those with dyslexia or other disabilities. Planning carefully, and adopting strategies to overcome any potential barrier to learning, is part of the challenge of being a student. Accepting help and advice in special circumstances is also part of the challenge, so use your strengths and work towards minimising your weaknesses.

Learning styles

The phrase 'learning styles' describes the way in which individual people acquire new knowledge and skills; it may already be familiar to you, as it is commonly linked to learning in the classroom and is based upon effective use of the five senses

Quick guide to learning styles

Read the descriptions of each style and tick the bullet points that suggest your behaviour. Generally, most people use a mix of learning styles, with one style appearing to be dominant over the others, so more ticks in one box may indicate your preferred learning style.

Learning style	Description	Like me?
Visual	■ Do you learn most when watching something or visualising pictures?	
	■ Do you say things such as 'I can just imagine . . .' and often use a visual vocabulary?	
	■ Do you test a spelling for a word by writing it down?	
	■ Do you like to gather information from pictures, drawings or charts, rather than listen?	
	■ Do you need to have everything in its proper place before you feel comfortable and ready to learn?	
Auditory	■ Do you readily engage in conversation and enjoy discussion and debate?	
	■ Do you recall conversations/names well?	
	■ Do you prefer oral instructions, rather than having to read them?	
	■ Do you say things such as 'It sounds like . . .'?	
	■ Do you talk to yourself as you learn (even mentally)?	
Kinaesthetic	■ Do you prefer doing something to reading or listening about it?	
	■ Do you prefer to jump in and get on with things?	
	■ Do you say things such as 'It felt good' or use other words associated with physical senses?	
	■ Would you like someone to show you how to do something rather than explain it?	
	■ Do you remember the things you have done, rather than things you have been told about or read about?	

to enhance learning. Learning styles are usually described as being 'visual', 'auditory' and 'kinaesthetic'. It is thought that different children learn in different ways, using different senses to stimulate brain function. Thus, some children learn when presented with information in a visual form, others learn through aural means and others through 'hands-on' experiences. The way a child learns using such senses is known as the 'preferred learning style'. Many school lessons are planned to contain elements of all three styles, in an effort to make learning accessible to all children. Simply put, each lesson will have something to see, something to hear and something to do. Adults too may have preferred learning styles. By becoming conscious of the ways in which you learn and putting this knowledge into good use in new situations, you may become more effective in the learning process. Detailed questionnaires are available on the internet, should you wish to investigate your learning style further.

Knowing your preferred learning style may help you in your study, as you can ensure that you use your favoured method to learn new things. If you are a kinaesthetic learner, you might choose to make the most of any opportunities to be physically active in your learning, by engaging in discussion or trying things out in a hands-on way. Similarly, if you know that you are a visual or an auditory learner you can opt for methods of study which use these learning styles. Alternatively, of course, you may find that you use all three learning styles in different learning situations! Whatever your learning style, you are probably well aware of those situations in which you learn well and others that you find more difficult. Use this information about yourself to create positive learning experiences as you engage in study, so as to help you learn in the most effective way.

Planning study time

When you first engage in a new period of academic study it is easy to feel that the study is taking over your life and that you are constantly under pressure. Working to assignment deadlines is one of the other main pressures of academic study. The first weeks are a very steep learning curve and you may feel that you have to be able do everything all at once. However, by knowing your preferred learning style(s) and systematically planning to develop your study skills, these problems may be reduced. Drawing up plans, and setting limits and targets, can break the study down into achievable goals and help you to retain a feeling of control. This in turn will make study more rewarding and enjoyable.

As a mature student you are likely to have a job, family and commitments that mean you are limited to part-time study. In this case, it is even more important that you help yourself by forward-planning so as to ensure that you can fulfil all your commitments and still have time to enjoy life! Take the opportunity at the start of your course of study to think about and establish a timetable and routine that will allow you to be in control of your learning and coursework. Later chapters offer examples of planning in specific academic areas, but it may be useful to consider the amount of time you have available for study at the beginning of your course. There will be indications in your course handbook of how much time you are expected to devote to academic work. Most mature students study on part-time courses that offer taught sessions, usually counted in units of six-hour days or evening sessions, which are then followed by independent study. The ratio of time between taught sessions and personal study is usually 1:3, i.e., for every hour taught, the student is expected to engage in about three hours of study. This time includes reading, research and academic writing of assignments. If your course has a taught input of 30 hours over eight weeks, you should expect to engage in independent study for at least a further 90 hours, making a total of 10–12 hours per week. How you will manage your time is a question of personal preference, but creating a timetable and a habit of regular study is worth considering at the outset.

Consider how you could plan out your week by deciding on how much time you have to study in between everyday tasks such as working, picking up the children, housework, relaxation and other activities that you wish to fit into the week. Create a timetable, taking account of the hours available, and plan your study time carefully. Use the timetable template on page 8 as a starting place to design your own timetable.

The example may not look realistic from your perspective – you may prefer to study early in the morning or late at night, or you may work best in short bursts or for longer periods of time. This is why you need to plan and work out your own system of study. It may look organised once you have your timetable recorded on paper, but there will be times when unexpected events intervene or you may be so busy that you forget to refer to the timetable during the week. It is a good idea to find out the procedures for late submission of work or for obtaining support in case you are unable to complete an assignment for any reason. Careful planning in one area, e.g. planning the week's shopping in advance, can free up time for study or relaxation. Not only will this gain precious time – it will eliminate one area of potential stress.

When managing time, it is particularly important to consider the effective use of the time set aside for study. List as many tasks as possible that you have completed over the last week or two, including household chores, family outings and those related to your work. Your list could be organised as shown in Figure 1.1 on page 10.

Some of the activities might be mundane and even boring, and others enjoyable and appealing. List what you spent most of your time doing and compare it with how you would prefer to spend your time. Are the two roughly equal? Many people complain that there is not enough time for the important things in life, and the not-so-important tasks that eat up time can increase stress levels. Careful planning and delegating of tasks will ease the stress and free up time to complete chosen activities. Share out the household tasks with family members, or plan to complete the tasks effectively in one go rather than spreading them out over time, e.g. make a list for the weekly shop so that you don't forget basics and have to go back for them!

You may discover that important things, such as quality time spent with family and friends, get pushed to one side as being self-indulgent or less important than

Weekly study/task timetable

	Morning (7am–12)	**Afternoon (12–5pm)**	**Evening (5–10.30pm)**
Monday			
Tuesday			
Wednesday			
Thursday			
Friday			
Saturday			
Sunday			

Try to be specific and realistic! Plan times when you can relax as well as study. Shorter times can be allocated for reading, or making notes. Some assignments may be due after the period of taught study. You will need to continue independent study during this time to complete the assignment task.

Timetable for longer period of study – to next assignment hand-in date

Tasks to be completed →	**Reading and planning**	**Writing and drafting**	**Tutorial dates: Hand-in date:**
Week 1			
Week 2			
Week 3			
Week 4			
Week 5			
Week 6			
Week 7			

Your completed timetable may look something like this:

	Morning (7am–12)	Afternoon (12–5pm)	Evening (5–10.30pm)
Monday	Work 8.00–4.00	At work	2 hours' study
Tuesday	Attend uni/college	Uni/college Visit library	Family evening
Wednesday	Work 8.00–4.00	At work	3 hours' study
Thursday	Work 8.00– 4.00	At work Weekly shop	3 hours' study
Friday	Work 8.00–4.00	At work	
Saturday			Family evening
Sunday			Family evening

Study plan for assignment

Tasks to be completed →	Reading and planning	Writing and drafting	Tutorial dates: Hand-in date:
Week 1	Check assignment details General research	Assignment plan structure	
Week 2	General reading General research	Draft introduction/ main points	Tutorial Tuesday
Week 3	Focused reading Workplace observations	Check plans Start to write	
Week 4	Focused reading Workplace observations	Write	
Week 5	Focused reading Re-check assignment details	Write	
Week 6	NO more reading! Proof-read assignment	Write	
Week 7		Check introduction and conclusion	Hand in next Tuesday.

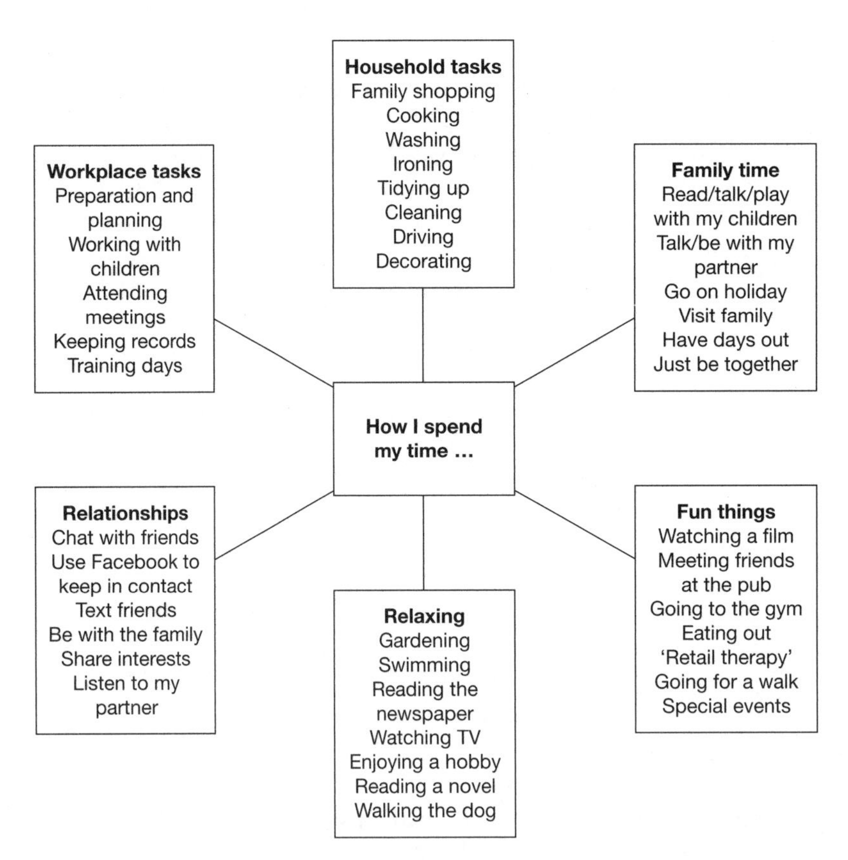

Figure 1.1 Everyday activities. This diagram lists examples of the everyday activities that may feature in your daily life. Which take up too much time and could be reduced through delegation or forward planning? Which are too important to miss out, and need to be 'ring-fenced' in your life?

other activities or even study. By planning well in advance, you can ensure a balance between time spent on activities that seem important and urgent and those which make life worthwhile. You may have got into a habit of doing things that are not really important – try to change some of your habits and free up time for other, more important aspects of your life. This should include spending time with friends and family as well as study!

When planning your study workload it is important to plan breaks. Evidence suggests that we remember and interpret information best if we take regular breaks, as this allows us to relax and facilitates the integration and absorption of ideas. It would seem that breaks of 5–10 minutes every 20–40 minutes produce the best relationship between understanding and recall. Consider also your style of learning – just sitting and reading silently is not necessarily the ideal way to learn. Decide whether discussing ideas with other students (by email or telephone), making notes of key words or ideas, watching a video or reading a book would be a more effective way to study.

Study tasks and study targets

One other aspect of time management is the use of study tasks. These are small, straightforward tasks that you can turn to if you find yourself becoming distracted or bored, such as:

- underlining significant ideas/quotations – you can use different coloured highlighter pens (but don't underline too much, as this can be confusing)
- making notes or drawing a mind map or spider diagram (see Chapter 2) for an essay/assignment/task that you have planned, as you work
- making a list of key points raised in your reading, listening or viewing
- reading a short specific section in a book in a given time – practise skimming and scanning
- constructing an essay plan as you work (see Chapter 4).

These tasks are not necessarily time-consuming but they will help you to focus your attention in a productive way.

Once you have created a timetable and considered your learning style, the questions of what to study and how to study arise. There are many reading resources, topics and interesting avenues of research, and making a choice in a limited time can be difficult. The determining factors for the decision might be drawn from the recommended reading lists and the assessment instructions, but even these will involve making decisions. Again, make a list for yourself of all the possible areas of study and then sort them out to help you in the decision-making process.

Obviously, you can engage the support of your tutor in making decisions, or share ideas with other students. Another idea might be to focus on and select areas for study by using the simple strategy of 'Plan, Do and Review' when preparing for and engaging in study (Figure 1.2).

By asking these types of questions before and after periods of study, you may find that you enhance your chances of success and enjoy a sense of achievement in completing the task as planned. From the first week of the course or module, check the stated learning outcomes and the assessment details, as these will give you clear indications of what you should be studying and learning. Another useful strategy might be to choose what you consider to be the hardest task first and to tackle it first, so as to give it more time, rather than to do the simple things first and worry about the real task later!

One of the traps that some students fall into when reading or studying is to find an item that is absorbing and interesting but not relevant to the overall purpose of the intended study. They may spend time investigating a new topic at the expense of relevant study time. If you have an assignment to complete to a deadline, then reduce the chances of falling into this trap by keeping the assignment brief clearly in front of you, and discipline yourself to stay on track. Create visual aids as reminders by copying out the essay question or the assignment wording in big

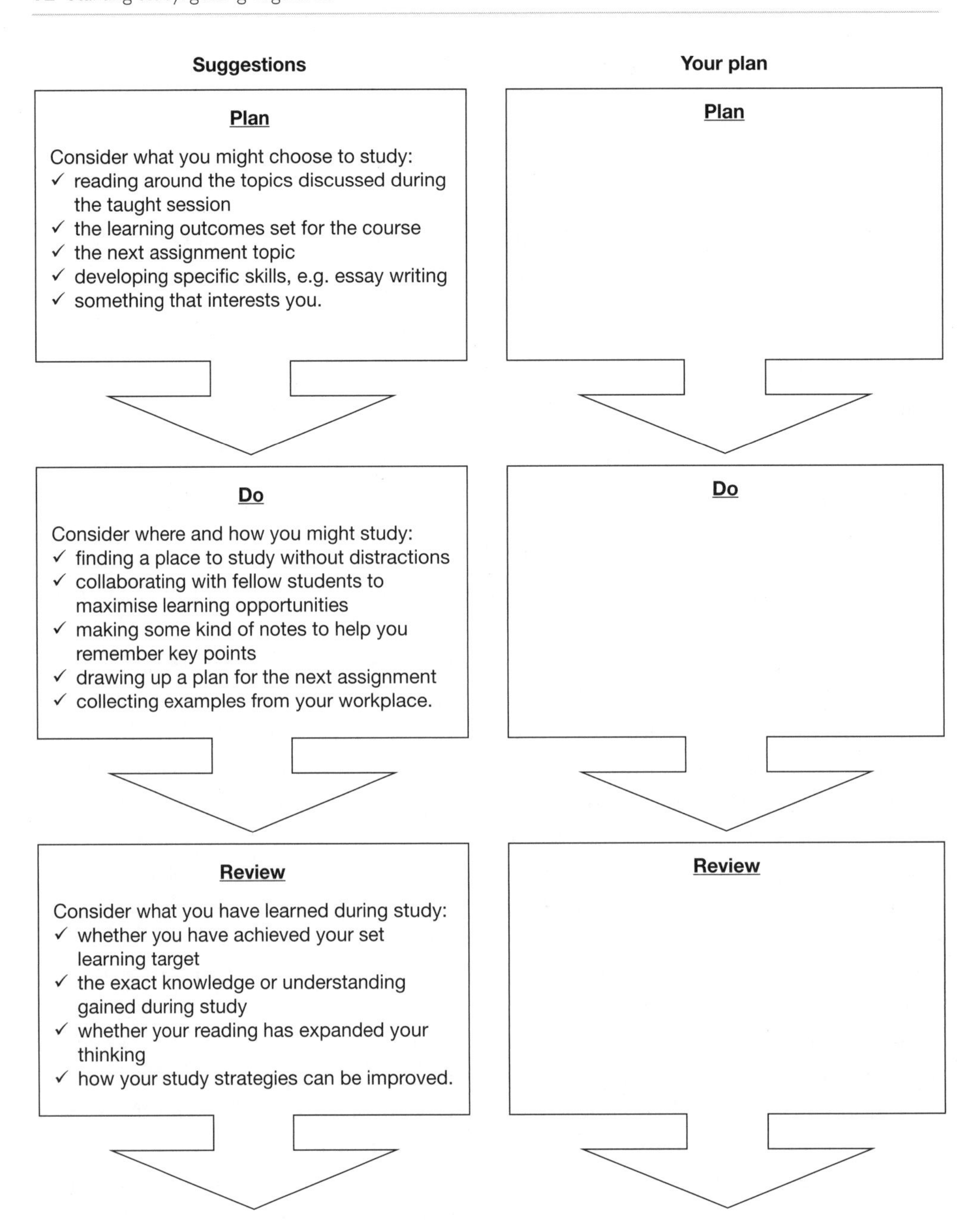

Figure 1.2 The 'Plan, do, review' process for setting study targets

letters. Your tutor will also supply a marking or assessment grid – keep this readily available, so that you know that you are working towards the criteria that have been set to pass the course. If you have an active rather than a passive relationship with your work, you will find it easier to utilise your study as a creative base from which to launch your own thoughts.

A drawback of all forms of target setting and similar focused planning is that you may block out or miss some potentially important areas by becoming too focused upon a narrow target. Although you should plan for study, there is sometimes an advantage to setting out on a voyage of relatively unplanned discovery. When your work is progressing well, then you can indulge in the luxury of 'browsing' by following up personal interests or wandering into unknown territories.

An environment for study

Where you study and at what time will obviously be determined by all kinds of factors, such as personal choice, children, space, social/professional commitments etc. It may seem obvious, but you will need to create a space in which to work. Where you study doesn't matter too much, as long as you are comfortable and free from interruptions. However, try to allocate somewhere that is not too comfortable, but with heat, light, fresh air and access to your books and files. If other members of the household are likely to disturb you, you may need to negotiate time to be alone.

Most of this chapter so far has focused on practical ways to organise study time and to set questions and targets so as to aid learning. As well as the ideas presented here, you may have thought of other ways to suit your own needs and personality. There is more to studying, however, than just developing practical skills. Perhaps the most important aspect of your approach to learning will be your own attitude and response to it – this cannot be reduced to brief advice, charts or simple suggestions. It may be linked intrinsically with your own experiences, attitudes to knowledge, authority and so on. It is also connected with how much importance you place on the work you are doing – not just the importance of passing an exam or gaining a degree, but a sense of significance and interest that will make study seem worthwhile for its own value. Your attention may not be gripped all the time, but you can still try to approach your work with an open mind and questioning attitude. This in itself will help you to gain the knowledge, skill and understanding that form the basic aims of all learning.

Part 2: introduction to study during taught sessions

Studying for assessment

Universities use different types of assessments to check that students are acquiring the knowledge, skill and understanding required for their chosen subject area. Although these may vary, the assessments often cause the most concern to new students. Therefore, it is advisable to become familiar with the measurement/grading tool used by your university or college. The assessment criterion is usually available in the form of a table or chart, but different forms of assessment may have different marking tables. The most usual forms of assessments that students are asked to complete are essays, written assignments, oral presentations, poster/display presentations, reports, case studies, independent enquiries and seen and unseen examinations.

The approaches to each type of assessment are given in later chapters. Although the assessments are all different, the approach to each should be the same. You may need to learn to appreciate the marking criteria and understand the learning outcomes for your course in order to be able to plan your study time effectively and work towards producing the required standard of work to pass the course. All of these expectations are built into study and success at HE level.

Lectures and discussion

Attending lectures, listening to tutors and others and discussing academic subjects are an important and visible part of university/college life. Tutors aim to provide students with the knowledge and understanding required in order to undertake independent study and then to pass the assessment for the course. Lectures form such an important part of HE practice that it is worth thinking about what the student has to do during the lecture. This may involve some multi-tasking, as you may have to simultaneously:

- follow the general argument/analysis of the lecturer
- understand the key points and specific examples and illustrations
- formulate questions in your mind and be ready to discuss the issues raised
- identify areas which need to be clarified, or references which you want to check
- make notes which reflect all of the above.

Lecturers may stimulate and inspire your interest in a new area of learning or give a new perspective to an old way of working. You may, however, feel that you have missed a point, or not understood all of what was said. You might consider the following strategies and choose appropriate ones to maximise your learning potential during lectures:

- Prepare for the subject in advance by reading, and have some questions in mind that you would like to have answered; become familiar with the names and work of key writers in the field.
- Be selective about what you write down, rather than trying to note everything down. Ensure that any notes you take will be easily understood by you at a later date.
- Use headings and sub-headings, mind maps, spider diagrams and so on, rather than extensive linear notes. Flexibility in the use of note-taking methods should make it more possible for you to capture the main ideas and strands of the lecture. Key words, author's names and significant details may be all that you need to capture in order to reconstruct the information later. Using the day's hand-out, and writing notes in the margin, or highlighting important parts as the tutor talks, may be just as effective.

- Some tutors provide hand-outs or PowerPoint presentation notes prior to the lecture to help you to prepare (or sometimes afterwards). Working through these again after the lecture may help you to fix the subject in your mind and can be a way to test your own understanding. It is also a good revision exercise.
- Try relaxing and just enjoying the subject. Someone else is doing most of the work, so allow your mind to follow what is being said. If you are tense and try to write down everything, you may miss the most important points!
- Making notes of references or names that you don't understand, so as to follow them up later, can give a focus to any extension work after the lecture. Many tutors allow time at the end when points and questions can be raised, but you should also be prepared to follow up some queries in the library.

Seminars, discussion and group work

Discussion is an important part of the academic process – providing students with an opportunity to listen to the views of others and to put forward their own ideas. You may not always agree with what someone else says, or may have different experiences to share. Often there is no 'right' answer – just a need to explore the issues. Do not be afraid to offer your opinion, or to challenge someone's view through carefully worded questions. Similarly, if someone challenges your argument, listen to what they have to say, and then respond to their points with evidence of your own experience or reading. This is particularly relevant when discussing work-based experiences, as you will have first-hand experience of your own workplace and will be able to compare your experience (whilst maintaining confidentiality!) with that of other students.

Checking your attitudes to others

During discussion, briefly examine your attitudes to the other students. This may help you to join in more freely

- Who seems to have authority? Who do you consider knows the most? Is this really true? Might they just be the loudest?
- Question what they say.
- Who uses their personal experiences to illustrate their views? Are their experiences the same as yours? Are they of equal value?
- Consider how you and others interpret experiences – do you all see things in the same way?
- What factual evidence or readings are used to support ideas? These may sometimes contradict each other, and then you may have to decide which one you agree with.

The purpose of discussion and debate is to help you to formulate your own ideas and to relate these to the experience and practice of others. Sharing ideas or following the research reading of fellow students may give you opportunities to note down book titles, websites and other reference material to follow up after the session. Discussion is an important part of the learning process, as it helps everyone to clarify their understanding and direct their individual learning. To take discussion further, it is important to develop informed opinions. Any independent study and reading that you have engaged in will be invaluable, as you can use this as evidence to support your views. Discussion is linked to the ability to think critically and question what you read and hear. If you are able to say, 'I think that because . . .', and give examples, it shows that you have explored the subject. If you have considered different points of view, evaluated any supporting reasons or evidence and come to a conclusion, then you can offer an informed opinion to the group. Asking questions shows respect for others by challenging them to think critically about their own beliefs and practices. This challenge and exploration is a vital part of discussion (see below).

As the course progresses, the discussion groups may become more focused – these are termed 'seminars'. You may be required to read and prepare information ready for discussion during a seminar, or to lead a group or take notes during discussion of a topic. This may sound daunting, but it is just an extension of the usual discussion group activities. Discussion, whether planned as seminars or spontaneous, should be lively, enjoyable and informative – so make the most of the opportunities!

Some ideas to help you approach discussion

- Try to be open-minded and listen to the viewpoints of others. You may not agree with what they say but you can respect their views.
- Always think and question ideas within yourself – be responsive to problems and challenges, not passive.
- Do not be afraid to be curious – explore, question, probe and ask for more details and evidence rather than be satisfied with sweeping statements or superficial explanations.
- Remember that you do not have to think the same way as everyone else.
- Try not to get caught up in the details. Stop occasionally to look at the 'bigger picture'.
- Get to know yourself. Think before the course day. What do you believe and know from your experience? Understand your own strengths and weaknesses and learn from others.
- Become involved and be enthusiastic! Try to get to the heart of the matter and really begin to understand the issues from several angles.

HANDY HINT

Preparing a reading for a seminar

Ask yourself:

Why is this book chapter/journal article/research paper important?
What is the publication date? Is the subject topical or out of date?
Is the author well known, or from a reliable, 'academic' background?
What questions are raised?
What evidence is used to support conclusions?
What are its implications for my workplace?
Can I find any faults/bias in the author's arguments?
Does it have any hidden agenda?

Developing study and graduate skills

Developing a range of study skills, including managing time and engaging in discussion, is a major part of university and college life and you may find that you are expected to plan, record and monitor your professional and personal development in specified skill areas. HE institutions may call such records 'Personal Development Plans' (PDP), and these are often evaluated by the student rather than marked as an academic piece of work. Tutors will, however, check progress regularly and offer supporting comments and ideas to help direct your studies. The PDP may be recorded as a portfolio, as an electronic record, or woven into the course structure.

The skills that are developed during study are referred to as 'Graduate Skills'. This term encompasses a broad spectrum of academic study skills, including those considered to be transferable or generic skills. Students will be expected to:

- have the ability to manage and improve their learning
- identify and overcome barriers to learning
- communicate, in speech and writing, the outcomes of learning
- work as part of a team
- use IT to assist learning and as a presentation tool.

These skills, valued by universities and employers alike, are seen as offering support in personal, professional and academic development. The transferable nature of many graduate skills is seen as a necessary requirement to allow for flexibility when facing changing workplace situations in the future. University and college departments offer support in developing these skills, often through online tutorials and guidance, but you can do much yourself just through reading and reflection and, of course, by being prepared to ask for advice and help when you feel that you need it.

Summary

This chapter may have raised some questions for you to answer about how, what and when you study. There have also been opportunities to:

- identify your basic learning style
- design a timetable to plan for study and consider priorities for study
- pose questions to direct your learning as you engage in personal study
- consider the use of assessment criteria to direct your study
- prepare for taught sessions, including lectures and discussion groups
- begin to develop a range of study and key skills.

By browsing the following chapters you may be able to identify which sections to read first to help you with your current studies, and note those which may help you at a later stage. As a mature student, you have many skills and experiences on which you can call. You should feel reassured when you spot similarities between what you already know and the expectations of academic study. Most of the 'rules' can be followed easily and will become routine with practice, but do not underestimate the worth of your own personal experiences and common sense in applying the rules in a way that makes the most of your own knowledge and abilities.

Further reading

- If you need to read more about any particular topic covered in this chapter, you might find that the best place to start looking is your own institution's resources. Your tutor will know which resources will be most helpful at this point in your studies, or you can check out the library or online resources. Simple key words may help with online searches, so start your search on your institution's web pages by looking for 'study guides', or 'graduate skills', or be more specific by searching for, e.g., 'study timetable'.
- HE students with dyslexia can find more information and advice from the British Dyslexia Association website (www.bdadyslexia.org.uk/).
- Theories related to 'learning styles' (aural, visual, kinaesthetic and others) can be located online. When searching for questionnaires to explore your own learning style, use those offered by universities.
- Publishers and authors offer many study resources. Search for items by:
  - Stella Cottrell (for general study skills)

- Skills4Study (Palgrave's website: includes audio study guides as well as PDF downloads)
- Stephen Covey (for time management)
- Tony Buzan (for mind mapping)
- Guy Claxton (for ideas on 'learning how to learn').

2 Reading for study

Introduction

This chapter concentrates on some of the skills associated with reading, in particular reading in the context of study. Reading is perhaps the most important aspect of learning – it not only provides information and argument but also gives structure to your imagination and influences your own style of writing. However, many students find this aspect of study difficult, sometimes because they are not used to reading 'academic' texts or because they have struggled with reading in the past. However, 'not reading' is never an option when approaching study! Adopting new ways of reading is a skill that requires consideration and practice in order to get the most out of academic texts.

The first part of this chapter concentrates on techniques for locating information, along with basic search strategies associated with reading. The latter part will begin to examine the finer points of reading, such as criticism, subtexts and the structure of argument. Further strategies designed to promote the successful location of appropriate and relevant reading materials are covered in Chapter 8.

Picking up a book

The title of this section may seem a little strange, but just picking up a book, especially a 'textbook', can be very daunting. This section suggests some ways to approach reading so that it is a productive and enjoyable experience.

First, consider how libraries categorise books and writing. For many people, reading a novel is a relaxing process which allows one to 'step into' the story. Newspapers can often seem a relaxing read too, although their value lies in the interest of the information and opinion they convey. On the other hand, books that are associated with study are seen as worrying – text to be 'got through' rather than enjoyed. A first step is to understand that there are different types of books and academic texts, and that you need to approach them in different ways. Developing academic reading skills will help you to use reading resources for study more effectively and with less anxiety.

Selecting and finding information

Studying often includes working through set texts or reading lists, but important information relevant to your topic need not necessarily come from textbooks. It can be found in a range of formats such as television documentaries, government statistics, reports, radio programmes, newspapers, CD-ROMs and the internet.

It is important to know how to find the most relevant information for your needs. This involves two processes: firstly, analysing your subject matter, and secondly, locating the book or information source that you require.

Analysing your subject matter

In order to find the right book, it might be useful to create a 'mind map' or 'spider diagram' of your subject and its related topics. This involves writing down everything relevant to the topic in a way described by Tony Buzan in one of his many books (see the bibliography at the end of this chapter). Quite simply, mind mapping is a way of sorting and recording thoughts. It can be used before starting study, or afterwards as a way of revision. Start a mind map by putting the main subject in the centre and noting down related key words as they occur to you.

For example, an assignment might be to write an essay related to 'parents and education' and this could be narrowed down to the topic of 'starting school'. Before writing, you will need to read around the subject. Your mind map may help to identify related topics in order to widen your search net. Look at this example of a mind map and how it extends the original idea of 'starting school'.

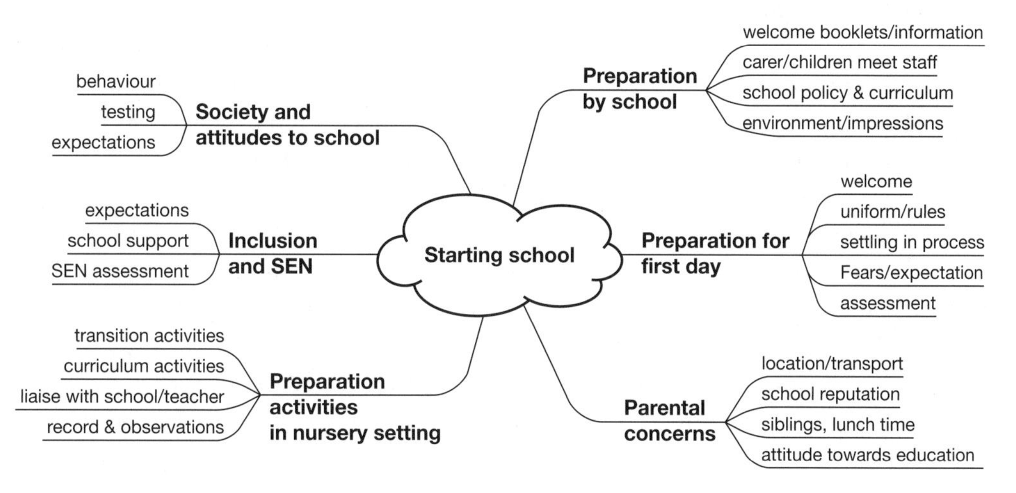

Figure 2.1 Example of a mind map

If you continue building this mind map, you will find that several other links can be made, using your experience and knowledge. You will then need to decide whether some of the links are connected to the focus of your study or if they are irrelevant to your present task. By planning in this way, you can use your study time effectively and identify areas that might be worth investigating further. If your library search does not immediately identify the texts that you are looking for, your tutor or librarian should be able to support you in finding the material that you need.

From your list, select key concepts that you will need to research, depending upon your role in the workplace. For example, if your workplace is a nursery setting, you might decide to give priority to these areas:

- preparation activities in the nursery setting
- making contacts with school
- attitudes to school and education
- expectations of teachers and parents.

When you have reduced your requirements to these essentials, you will need to expand them again by considering alternative words or phrases which mean almost the same thing. For example, 'nursery setting' may also be described as pre-school education, or early years or foundation stage settings. When you start to search for reading material, your chances of finding what you need will be greater if you have considered alternative phrases in common use (see Chapter 8). Now that you have a clearer idea of the topic and its related key words, you will need to identify and locate the appropriate material. Libraries and the internet have 'search engines' to help you to locate reading resources. For example, a search for 'starting school' and 'early years' in one library catalogue retrieved the items shown in Figure 2.2.

In such a list, you might find books that are useful but not quite what you are looking for. You can then choose whether to start a new search using your other key words, or to locate similar books on the library shelf by noting the class mark. In the list, you can see that three books have a similar class mark starting with the digits 372. If you look on the library shelves for this number you will find more books on the same subject. Note that other class marks show that books on the subject are located on different shelves of the library, or are even online as e-books. By searching the library catalogue online prior to visiting the library, you will be able to locate books with comparative ease when you visit the library building.

Once you have found relevant book titles, you can start reading. However, other information may also be found in social history sources such as newspaper reports, articles in educational journals and government reports. You can search for these in a similar way in the library or on the internet by using key words related to your topic.

The library catalogue may also give you further information about location or availability. Note too, that the library catalogue lists resources by authors' last names together with date of publication. Latest publications are listed first!

Author's name	**Book title**	**Date of publication**	**class mark – for location**
Hill, Malcolm	Children's services: working together: professionals working together with the community	2012	362.7 CHI
O'Connor, Anne	Understanding transitions in the early years: supporting change through attachment and resilience	2012	155.423 OCO
Callan, Sue	Work-based research in the early years	2011	e-Book
Fisher, Julie	Moving on to Key Stage1: improving transition from the early years foundation stage	2010	e-Book
Fisher, Julie	Moving on to Key Stage1: improving transition from the early years foundation stage	2010	372.21
Brooker, Liz	Starting school: young children's learning cultures	2002	372.1829 BRO
Fabian, Hilary	Children starting school: a guide to successful transitions and transfers for teachers and assistants	2002	372.241 FAB

Figure 2.2 Making sense of library catalogue search results

Locating information

Libraries

You might think that all libraries are the same; places where you can get books. However there are different types of libraries: public libraries, academic (schools, colleges and universities), research libraries, business libraries.

Libraries organise their collections by giving every book a class mark – the number on its spine. This number determines where the book is located within the library. It is important for you to know how to identify and locate material in the library, as colleges and universities often have vast collections of specialised books. This is where the library catalogue is an invaluable tool.

A library's catalogue is a list of all the material held in that library. This includes videos, software, curriculum resources, music CDs, newspapers and journals, as well as books. Libraries have computerised catalogues. You do not need to search the shelves for the books that you need, but you can search through the online catalogue, as previously explained (often in the comfort of your own home if you

HANDY HINT

Distance learners

UK Libraries Plus is a joint enterprise between many universities that allows students to borrow books from other university libraries that may be closer to home.

Or, you could try your local public library (check its online catalogue and services on offer) to see what resources are available.

Also, check out local charity book shops close to universities or buy second-hand books from other students!

have internet facilities). This will allow you to carry out some preliminary research before reserving the books online for collection when you visit the library.

The catalogue is organised in a way that makes cross-referencing easier. Lists can be organised in any number of different ways – alphabetically by author, alphabetically by title, chronologically, by subject. Each of these methods of arrangement has its uses. Library catalogues facilitate the accessing of information by using a range of different methods. Whether you are looking for works written by a specific author, or works on a specific subject, the library catalogue will enable you to find it quickly and easily.

Many books are now available electronically and can be read online anywhere that there is internet access. Your institution will have a growing number of e-books available as part of its e-library. Others can be located through search engines such as Google Scholar. With so many available reading resources it is even more important to prepare a search strategy so as to avoid being overwhelmed by the volume of material (see more in Chapter 8).

Finding articles in journals

Some libraries refer to journals as 'periodicals'. Don't be put off by this, as they are the same thing – collections of academic articles published in scholarly magazines. While library catalogues are useful for locating materials such as books, CDs and DVDs, they are unlikely to provide detailed information about the content of journals. In order to supplement your reading with relevant journal articles, you will need to use an e-library database and consult the indexes or abstracts. Every library subscribes to e-journals and you will need your library card or password in order to access and read the full text of e-journals online. Figure 2.3 shows what a journal reference looks like, giving you all the information that you will need in order to find the journal in the library or online.

An abstract is a summary of the content of an academic book or a journal article. HE libraries provide bound copies of abstracts (or you can read them online) as a means of locating articles, rather than browsing through the journals themselves.

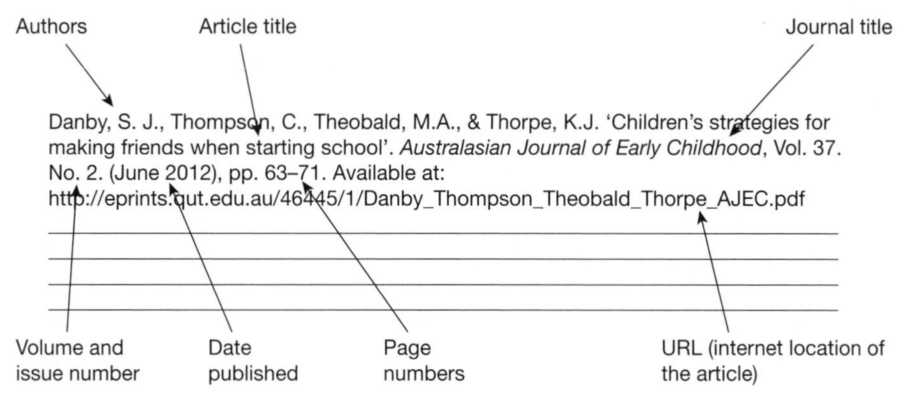

Figure 2.3 Example of a bibliographic entry

Example of a journal abstract

Australasian Journal of Early Childhood, Vol. 37, No. 2, 2012, pp. 63–71

Children's strategies for making friends when starting school

Danby, S. J., Thompson, C., Theobald, M.A., and Thorpe, K.J., Queensland University of Technology

ABSTRACT: Starting school is a critical and potentially stressful time for many young children, and having supportive relationships with parents, teachers and peers and friends offers better outcomes for school adjustment and social relationships. This paper explores matters of friendship when young children are starting school, and how they initiate friendships. In audio-recorded conversations with a researcher and their peers, the children proposed a number of strategies, including making requests, initiating clubs and teams, and peer intervention to support a friend. Their accounts drew on social knowledge and relational understandings, and showed that having someone, a friend, to play with was important for starting school. Children gave serious attention to developing strategies to initiate friendships.

Key words: friends, early childhood, research interview, peer culture, child-initiated

The abstract gives all the information needed to find the full text. After reading the abstract, you can decide if the article might be relevant to your study or not. Note too, the list of key words.

By reading the abstract, you can decide whether the full text of the article is likely to give you the information that you require. Some journals may be borrowed from the library; however, most articles are now available for reading online and are easily located using their URL. Their availability online offers greater flexibility, as they can be searched using key words.

It is important to search effectively in order to obtain relevant information – quality is far more important than quantity. Your tutors will not be impressed if you cite 30 inappropriate/irrelevant articles in your work. It is important to select articles that are highly relevant to your needs. Developing good searching skills will enable you to sort out the wheat from the chaff and avoid huge photocopying/printing bills and hours spent reading irrelevant articles. Many libraries offer training sessions in the use of the library catalogue and on researching online journals. These are well worth attending, but for quick reference here are the main points of carrying out a search. More search strategies can be found in Chapter 8.

HANDY HINT

A quick overview of search tips

- Decide your search terms – make a list of alternative ways of saying the same things.
- Look at the publication year – do you just want very recent material?
- Who wrote it? Is this a name that you recognise?
- Has anything else been written on the subject since this was published?
- What level is it aimed at? (General public, undergraduate, post-graduate)
- If it is a journal, is it available in the library, as an online journal article, or will you have to obtain it on inter-library loan?
- If you find too many articles, then narrow your search parameters – use Boolean logic search strategies (Chapter 8).
- If you do not find enough, then broaden the search with new key words and phrases. Don't give up – try several search terms and different databases.

Searching bibliographies

Another useful place to look for help is in the books or articles themselves. Most books and articles have a suggested reading list or a bibliography at the end. A bibliography is a list of books and articles that the author has used in writing the text or considers useful to the topic under discussion. Sometimes the bibliography is organised around key themes or related to particular chapters. Bibliographies are arranged alphabetically by authors' names. They can be valuable sources of information. Some subject bibliographies are available on internet websites.

Using the internet

The internet is an invaluable source of information from around the world and you may be able to find the information that you require on one of the many websites. However, do check the date and source of such information carefully, to ensure that it is relevant, and remember that anyone can post information on a web page and it may not always be accurate. Use a tool such as the 'Internet Detective' to help you to determine the value of the material you have located.

Browsing

Browsing along bookshelves or through the pages of book, scanning for references and ideas on where to look for further information are all part of being an active reader and a good student. Exploring a subject in this way should also enable you to get some idea of its development and contours. For example, you can reflect upon:

- how much is written on a particular topic (*Are there too many books to choose from or not enough?*)
- when was it written (*Is it recent, or too old to be relevant?*)
- what themes have been developed/ignored (*Does it cover what you need?*)
- who are the key authors in the field (*Does the same name keep coming up?*)

These are vital steps in understanding your subject and therefore in beginning to know where to search for the information you require.

Types of reading

If you follow your plan, you should be able to find appropriate books for your topic of study, so now consider the way in which you will read them. Students rarely have to read an entire book to find the information that they need – perhaps just a chapter will be relevant, or sometimes even less. Academic reading is in part about dipping into lots of different texts. Much has been written about reading – e.g. speed reading, reading more efficiently, skimming and scanning text and so on, and you may want to pursue these techniques through further reading of your own. It is useful to think about different techniques for reading and how you can develop them as you study. Four types of reading are described below.

- Receptive – this is the sort of reading that we use most frequently. It is close to simply *listening* to the author (as when we're absorbed in a novel). Reading like this is characterised by its ease and steady pace, making it enjoyable.
- Reflective – this requires us to think very carefully about what we're reading, i.e. we need to reflect on it. This approach will involve analysing and weighing up ideas and information. When reading reflectively, we have to pause to think about what we have just read, and consider its meanings and implications. This is a good way to approach academic reading, as it encourages you to take things slowly, grasping and retaining the argument before moving on.
- Skimming – this is a much faster way of reading but it can be equally useful in study. Running your eyes over a page will give some idea of what is in a text, but not necessarily of what it means. It will give the gist of the text, how the ideas are organised and the types of examples that are included. Most academic books are structured to make the information easy to access. Read the opening

paragraph, the first and last sentences of some paragraphs and the conclusion. This should give you an overview of a whole chapter very quickly.

- Scanning – when you *scan* a page, your eyes and brain work together seeking particular words, phrases or ideas. One obvious everyday example of scanning is looking up a telephone number in a directory. Most people can locate words and associated words with an almost unconscious ease – the eyes travel rapidly over the page and the brain locates groups of letters which form the required word. All this takes just a few seconds. In an academic context this is particularly useful when looking for a reference to an author, event or title.

HANDY HINT

When you first open a book . . .

1 Check the contents – can you find what you need in this book?
2 Check the index – does it contain the key words that you have identified?
3 Explore the introduction and conclusion for the chapter(s) that looks most relevant. These parts of the text often contain the central ideas of the chapter and may be particularly useful when deciding which books or parts of the book are worth a closer study.
4 Remember: to find the information that you need, you do not have to read the whole book!

One very useful approach which combines skimming and scanning is to read through the first four sentences of each paragraph in a chapter, section or page. This often gives a good idea of the themes that are developed more fully in the rest of the text, providing a useful structure for notes and a quick way of getting the gist of a piece of writing. If you are working from your personal copy of the book, or from a photocopy, you may wish to highlight key phrases for future reference. Alternatively, consider reading the opening section of a chapter and then the conclusion, as this will also quickly give you an overview of the whole chapter. These approaches may also prompt some questions to direct your reading further, as suggested below.

HANDY HINT

Reading for information

- Approach the text with specific questions in mind. Three questions offer a good starting point. Answer these as you read – this will help you to be selective in what you read and to extract the most meaning and value from it.
- Use more than one resource, and select those which will be most helpful and relevant to your study
- Keep an open mind about what you read. Your time will probably be limited, so concentrate on reading set texts first (but not exclusively). Reading around

HANDY HINT

a topic can be informative and enjoyable and can stir your interest in the subject.

- Check the bibliographies of the books, journals or articles that you read – they may indicate other texts that you would find useful
- Check the date of what you are reading. Do not rely entirely on older textbooks, but generally go for texts published within the last five years or so. (Of course, some 'classic' texts NEVER go out of date!)

Read on . . .

Having considered various techniques and approaches to reading, now look at reading from a different, perhaps deeper level. This approach will involve looking for the structure and style of a text, its hidden meanings, how to uncover them and how to follow the argument and intention of the author. Only by regular reading will you be able to make sense of the information and guidance presented; you should try to get into the habit of reading, for pleasure as well as for study.

More than any other aspects of study, reading will form your experience as a student. Through reading you will learn more about your subject, and more about how to write, think and judge. This chapter is geared towards academic reading, but the principles within it can be usefully applied to all sorts of text, from novels to technical manuals. So read on!

Purpose in reading

The reader's purpose

The purpose of reading is not only to gather information but also to develop your understanding, to weave together new ideas with new knowledge and to introduce new perspectives into your thinking. In other words, reading shouldn't be seen as a mechanical process or a chore, but as a way of stretching your thoughts and imagination.

This aspect of reading should not be bypassed, otherwise the underlying learning process will be impeded. Learning is to do with changing your ideas, combining them in new ways and extending them to cover new ground and different ways of looking at them. Reading a text is one of the most important ways in which you can trigger these changes. So, reading is vital to learning!

The purpose of reading is *not* to have a lot of words pass in front of your eyes, *nor* to add more items to the long list of information that you already have in your memory, but rather, it is to clarify your ideas and make you rethink them. Reading should be active, not passive, creative, an exploration – and should involve your critical judgement of what is written.

The writer's purpose

Active reading involves interaction with the text and, implicitly, with the author. When you sit down to read a book or a chapter you are entering into a relationship with its writer. Start by trying to discover the purpose of the text and give some thought to the writer's intentions. This will help you to understand the text more fully – to see it in context and to grasp its meaning more easily. There are many clues that help you to categorise the intentions of a writer. One approach is to look at the location of a text:

- Is it in a book, newspaper, journal or magazine? What is known of the background, politics and audience of the publication will affect the expectations of the reader. A tabloid newspaper such as the *Sun* or the *Daily Mail* will promote a different sort of writing to a broadsheet paper such as *The Times*. And *The Times* will provide a different sort of argument to, say, the *Guardian*. Journalistic writing also has its own particular priorities: it has to be eye-catching (with headlines and headline puns), to the point, relatively short and readable.
- Is it an academic text? Likewise, academic writing has a particular style. Such writing has to cope with a large number of complex and abstract ideas which often arise from very detailed and specific information. As a result, academic writing has its own vocabulary and style and follows certain rules, usually determined by the subject matter. Subjects are described as 'disciplines' partly because of their accompanying rules related to style, choice of vocabulary, evidence, etc. These rules become more apparent by reading the text.
- Is it old or new? If it's old – what is its background? When and why was it written? How does it 'fit in' with modern text? From what period does it come? Different periods of history have quite different values and priorities. Imagine reading a book describing education in the 1930s or 1970s. How would its concerns be different to those of today?

Categorising texts

Another way to make sense of texts is to place them into the following categories, which are basic but useful as a rule of thumb:

- Narrative: a piece of writing that relates a series of events such as a story or history.
- Expository: a text that explains something.
- Argumentative: a text that reasons, gives an argument and tries to convince the reader that one method or process or belief etc. is correct.
- Satirical: a text that attacks someone or something using humour and irony.

Most texts will fall into more than one of these categories but many will be predominantly of one sort or another. Having some idea of the writer's purpose makes it easier to follow their approach to a subject and to be sensitive to the tone and structure of their writing. For example, a piece of narrative writing is often descriptive and straightforward. It moves through events and creates an interest in what might happen next. Traditionally, narrative has a resolution – an ending that closes the story. Argumentative texts, on the other hand, are often more demanding. You may need to follow the connections more closely and be open to ideas as well as information. Often argumentative pieces are left open-ended – almost demanding a response or a development of the ideas they contain.

Reading critically

A philosopher called Cornelius Castoriadis once wrote that reading was like holding a conversation with the dead. This is particularly true of old texts. You may not be able to question an author, but this doesn't mean that you should accept everything you read as being correct – even academics get things wrong, and, perhaps more importantly, information may be omitted. Events, people and ideas may get forgotten because they have not been included in the written accounts of a subject. It is important to think about what is missing from the text you are reading as well as what it does contain, whatever the date of production.

One way of reading critically and creatively is to pose questions of the text; asking questions and finding answers is what makes reading productive and interesting. While you read a text, keep some questions at the back of your mind, such as:

Reading critically (1): weighing up the argument

- Do I like/agree with the author's position and views?
- Do I believe their argument?
- What other approaches are there to this subject?
- Is their position biased, and what form does the bias take?
- Is the evidence presented sufficient to support their argument?

These are questions that weigh up the argument or opinion in a text.

Reading critically (2): assessing the style

- How easy is it to read this text? Does it flow easily?
- Is it too technical? Too abstract? Too wordy?
- How does the author use language to emphasise some parts or lead the reader to given conclusions?
- How am I affected by the language/imagery of this text?
- What metaphors are used to explain important points?

These are questions which address the language and style of the text

Of course, questions about language and style also have an effect on argument, and vice versa. Sometimes the questions that you frame in your mind whilst reading will be of a very general and open nature: 'Am I convinced by this?' or 'Is this what my own experience tells me?' Sometimes they will be of a particular kind: 'Has the author covered all the points or provided a convincing piece of evidence?' In either case, questions help the reader to feel involved with the text, to read actively.

Questions are important. Whilst you are asking questions of the text it is, in a way, asking questions of you: 'Do you follow my line of argument?' 'Do you agree with what I'm saying?' Most authors question the subject or events about which they are writing. If you are finding it difficult to get involved with what you're reading it is probably because you can't identify the questions being asked or what questions *you* should be asking. You may need to stop reading, look at the Preface or the Introduction of the book or 'skim' a few other chapters – then you can try to begin reading actively again!

If the reading is more technical it may help to use a dictionary or a thesaurus. You could also try reading a different text, based on the same subject, to clarify terms or to find alternative meanings. Anything that helps you to form questions relevant to the subject of the text is going to be helpful.

HANDY HINT

When you can't get into the text!
Some things cannot be hurried! It may help to put the book down and find something else to do. Let the issues rest on the 'back-burner' of your mind and see if a little time and relaxation will assist.

Sometimes even taking longer and 'sleeping on the problem' will provide some answers.

Do not be afraid to reject a book because its style or language does not appeal to you. There are usually plenty of other texts dealing with the same subject matter from which to choose.

Understanding the structure of a text

Most authors are trying to convey one or two central ideas – these are the underlying ideas of a text that are often supported by examples, comparisons or the reiteration of established ideas and so on. Understanding these underlying ideas is critical to understanding and evaluating the author's argument. Once they have been identified, you can then compare the author's ideas with your own and with the ideas of others in the field. Overall, you will be seeking to weigh up the author's view and develop from it your own intellectual position and values. You can help yourself in this by being aware of the structure of the argument or narrative that you are reading.

Ideas and meanings are the vital parts of a text. Some ideas will be argued openly, using illustrations and direct information; others will be implied (using innuendo, humour, suggestion). Sometimes what *isn't* written will tell us most about the position of the author. Other important elements are:

- the language of a text – its choice of words, metaphors, images
- the structure of a text – how ideas are arranged and connections made between ideas.

The following guidelines will help you to be aware of these elements whilst reading:

- Pause often to think about what you have read. What are the stated arguments? What are the underlying ideas?
- Look at the choice of examples or illustrations. Is anything excluded or distorted? What is emphasised? Are there sufficient references to evidence? Does the detail of the text support the argument or detract from it?
- Look at the language the author uses. Is it designed to provoke feeling in the reader? Is it over-detailed, sentimental, too complex, muddled or technical? Is it clear, to the point, expressive, appropriate? In other words, does it work? If not, why not?
- Think about the organisation of the argument. How are points arranged? Is only one side of an argument presented? Are ideas argued through, or simply stated? Are there any contradictions in the argument?

Following an argument

Following an argument is often the most important and the most difficult aspect of academic reading. Sometimes it is as much as we can do to make sense of what is written; going further, to the stage of critically understanding the line of argument that an author is making can seem too difficult. Here is a short-cut method that may help you in the initial stages.

HANDY HINT

Following an author's argument

Authors often use topic sentences. These are sentences that indicate the substance of what follows in a paragraph or section of writing. They are usually found at the beginning of paragraphs, or sometimes at the end of the preceding paragraph. Finding topic sentences is a useful way of following an author's argument.

Consider also the length or range of an argument. A book may have several areas of concern, and these are often represented by different chapters, sections, subsections and so on. Likewise there may be many lines of argument running through the text. These might be quite separate and related to different topics, or they might interconnect, presenting different aspects of one large thesis. Be aware of the parameters of your reading matter. Are you reading a whole article, or a chapter, or are you reading only part of one of these? Are you reading about a particular topic and no further? Is what you are reading part of an ongoing and developing argument?

It may help to recap on some of the ideas already covered in this section:

- You need to have a good idea of what the author is trying to convey. Use a dictionary to check meanings and refer to the footnotes for references. Take account of the context of the text, its age, intended audience etc.
- Try to follow the sequence of ideas. Most argument will follow the basic principles of logical thought, i.e. one idea will follow on from the other as a development of the previous idea.
- As critical readers, our job is not only to follow the argument and make sense of it but also to judge it, to decide for ourselves whether it is well put together or not. To do this we need to look for the backbone of the text, to distinguish between facts and opinions, to examine the evidence put forward, to look at the nature of the language and illustrative language used.

Précis and comprehension

One of the best ways to develop your sense of the language, structure and argument within a text is an exercise called précis. A précis is a summary or abstract of a passage (the term comes from the French for 'precise' or 'accurate'). The chart below shows you how this can be done, stage by stage.

How to précis or write an abstract

1	2	3
1 Read the passage thoroughly, so as to understand and appreciate it. Use a dictionary to look up words you don't understand.	2 Note the stages of the argument. What sequence is given to the points made? Can you identify three (or more) main points?	3 Note the way in which the argument is supported. Try to be general in your version – don't be too detailed. Avoid any stylistic use of repetition, questions and so on.

4 Now, summarise in your own words what you have read, perhaps in rough form first, remembering to:

- Leave out examples, illustrations and any unnecessary details.
- Group ideas together into 'clumps' so that you can see the development of the stages of the argument.

Alternatively, rather than working in the linear way suggested in Figure 2.13, you could start a mind map as you read the text and then use this as a prompt for a summary of the main points. Whichever method you choose, the experience should help you to get the most out of your reading.

Summary

This chapter has looked briefly at some of the skills associated with reading, many of which you may already use quite naturally, and others that you may have to work harder at in order to develop. Although practising these skills in the early stages of study may seem time-consuming, it will prove worthwhile in the long term. Ultimately, the choice is yours – if one author's style does not suit you, then find an alternative.

Further reading

Books and articles that are designed to develop academic reading skills:

- Authors:
  - John Langan
  - Sarah Philpot
  - Stella Cottrell (also Palgrave's online study skills website Skills4study)
- Internet Detective is an online tool designed to help students to identify reliable internet sources: http://www.vtstutorials.ac.uk/detective/index.html.
- The Open University and other university websites provide resources that are reliable and trusted to support academic reading skills.
- Try a key words search online for tutorials in those areas that you find particularly challenging.

3 Note taking

Introduction

This chapter will look at the reasons why it is important to take notes and some of the variety of ways by which you can do this – for example, by marking the page, identifying key words, linear and non-linear notes. It will also consider ways of filing and using notes.

Note taking is an important extension of reading. The information and ideas that you encounter in your reading need to be recorded and absorbed, and note taking helps you to do this. However, like many skills, there are ways in which to improve, and some suggestions are given in this chapter. An active reader should also be an active note taker, as notes should provide an opportunity to rethink and develop the material you are studying. Note taking is also an important skill when listening to lectures, in order to record key facts, or when observing children in the workplace, and so the ideas given in this chapter can be adapted for use in situations other than reading.

Why take notes?

The primary purpose of taking notes is to aid memory. Whether the notes are taken from a lecture, a book or something like a film or television programme, they will form a central part of your study and you will have to invest a great deal of time in them. However, it is important to remember that you can't hope to retain everything that you read, hear or discuss; instead, consider how to make notes that will remind you of the most important items. What is included should be enough to reconstruct the rest of the material, or at least to enable you to locate material that you may need in the original texts.

It can be tempting to use note taking as a replacement for learning. However detailed the notes are, they will mean nothing when you return to them unless you have understood the material in the first place and incorporated this understanding into your notes. Notes that are just a copy or a summary may mean nothing when you return to them at a later date.

A better way to view the process is to see note taking as an opportunity to reorganise and reorder the information contained in the original, and thereby to understand the material better, to clarify meanings and to apply your interpretation and criticism.

Note taking: self-assessment

Notes as a point of reference

One of the most important aspects of note taking is the use of notes as a source of reference in later study and essay writing. You will want to look back on notes that you make now, and in the days, weeks or months ahead. You may want to use them for essays, research, reports or exam revision. You may find them useful as a starting point for more detailed study. In any event, it is important that you can:

- find the notes
- read them and make sense of them
- locate their source (this is important for referencing and bibliographies).

It is tempting to forget the details when you get absorbed in the meaning of the text, but for obvious reasons always write the details of the source at the beginning of your notes:

- The title of the book/e-journal article/written text. If it is an article, include the title of the article and the title of the journal/newspaper/book that it came from. One way of making sure that you keep the bibliographic details of a book is to photocopy the title page when you first use the book in the library and make your notes on the back of the photocopy. This way you will have notes and a visual image of the book to trigger your memory when you revisit your notes.
- The title of a film, radio or TV programme. As with books, note the key details, including the date of production or transmission, the date when you listened or watched, along with any other relevant information. Sometimes it is possible to download a transcript for a film, radio programme or TV documentary and this can be useful as a basis for note taking.
- The author/lecturer. Again, if the material is an article or an essay, include the author/editor of the publication it comes from, as well as the name of the author of the article.
- Date of lecture. If you are using a set of PowerPoint presentation slides or notes given to you by the tutor, then record your notes down the side of the page, including any discussion points. It is often worth looking at such notes again after the lecture and adding other supporting information, such as book or journal articles or workplace examples that illustrate key points.

- Page numbers. Record the page numbers in the margin or by the side of key points. This is especially important if you intend to make reference to or quote an author – you will have to give a page number in the reference.

  In addition to the above:

- Make a note of cross-references, where appropriate. If you think of another piece of writing, an idea or an argument that is relevant to what you are reading, add it to your notes.
- File your notes. It is important that you know where to find notes on a particular topic, so work out a filing system that suits you at the beginning of study. You may want to keep an electronic bibliography that records authors' details and the key points of texts. These can then be listed alphabetically by author or by topic. As a general rule, it is best to use these as a supplement to fuller notes. Alternatively devise a simple collection grid for your note taking, or keep brief records in a small notebook.

Note-taking skills assessment

Where are you starting from? Mark yourself out of ten on the following note-taking skills.

I am able to:

1 Extract important information when listening or reading. ....

2 Recognise the difference between main and supporting points. ....

3 Incorporate my own analysis of the material. ....

4 Clearly register and record what is my own thought and what is not. ....

5 Use a variety of note-making techniques. ....

6 Use my notes as a source of reference or revision. ....

7 Present information so that it can be used later and for other purposes. ....

How did you do?

Look at the points you have awarded yourself for each question. You should be able to spot your strengths and weaknesses easily from the individual scores, and highlight the areas to work on.

Between 7 and 10: Excellent, you feel confident in this area.

Between 4 and 6: Fairly confident, but consider if you can develop further.

Below 3: You should develop and use this skill more often to become confident when making notes.

Like many self-assessment tools, this will only give you an idea of your own perception of your note-taking abilities. You might be too tough or too soft on yourself!

Activity:

You could make this assessment more reliable by reading a passage and making notes and then asking someone else to assess your capabilities by marking against the criteria listed above. The question then would be, do you trust their judgement?

Notes as an aid to understanding

As indicated in Chapter 2 on reading, most authors have a limited number of key points that they wish to make. These may be points of information, argument or query. In note taking, as in reading, it is important to be able to pick out the key points or the bare bones of whatever you are studying.

Uncovering and understanding the central theme or argument of a piece of writing, or a lecture, can be a really gratifying experience. It helps you to feel that you are getting somewhere and are not just at the receiving end of a lot of information. Once you have grasped these key points there is little need to record in elaborate detail all the information or ideas that were used to support them. It is a good idea to see note taking as an opportunity to be selective. Choose what information to include, and concentrate on the central arguments. For example, read the passage below and select the key words and phrases that give you the overall meaning of the text, before reading the next paragraph.

Asking effective questions

Looking for the key points. Identify the key words or ideas in this passage.

Generally, everyone loves asking questions, but not everyone is so keen on answering them, particularly in an academic or testing situation. It is worth considering why this is so, and then listening to the type of questions that you ask children.

First, there is the fear of giving the wrong answer. This is particularly true of questions that appear to have only one answer, for example: 'How many tens are there in one hundred?' or 'What colour is the sky?' Anyone with a number phobia will not wish to answer the first question, and the second question seems so simple that it might be a trick and you might be made to look foolish! For the adult working with children, this means that when asking closed questions only a small number of children will be able to participate before the 'right' answer has been found. These closed questions therefore have limited use when you are trying to promote a range of responses and debate. Open questions, such as, 'How many ways can you make one hundred?' or 'Do you wonder why the sky is blue?' are more likely to encourage a variety of responses that extend thinking and raise further opportunities for children to ask questions and problem-solve. Learners responding to open questions are also more likely to recognise that their responses are of value and will therefore feel encouraged to continue.

Of course, closed questions do have a place and can be a useful way of checking understanding and knowledge, but to build confidence in children and extend thinking, ask open questions or, better still, encourage the children to ask the questions. It has been said that young children are naturally inquisitive and continually ask questions, but this seems to fade away once they start school. So, use other ways to encourage children to pose questions: create mind maps, introduce a 'question box', perform interviews and set problems that promote questioning. All these activities will enable children to grow in confidence when asking and answering questions.

Your list of key words/phrases might include the following: effective questioning, confidence, open and closed questions, extend thinking, supporting adult.

The idea of key words is important here. Key words or phrases will stand out as significant in a piece of writing. They may be words that summarise or encapsulate an idea, or that jog your memory about information or arguments. You will also find that key words are important in creating *mind maps* or *spider diagrams* to help you with your learning. Mind mapping was devised by Tony Buzan. Creating a mind map starts with the main topic or theme, which you write in the centre of the page. You then add lines that branch out from the centre and words that are suggested by the main topic. For example, a mind-mapping set of notes based upon the paragraph above might start off as shown in Figure 3.1.

This can be further developed by adding new ideas, writing along the lines rather than at the ends of the lines. So, still inspired by the ideas contained in the reading, the mind map might develop as shown in Figure 3.2.

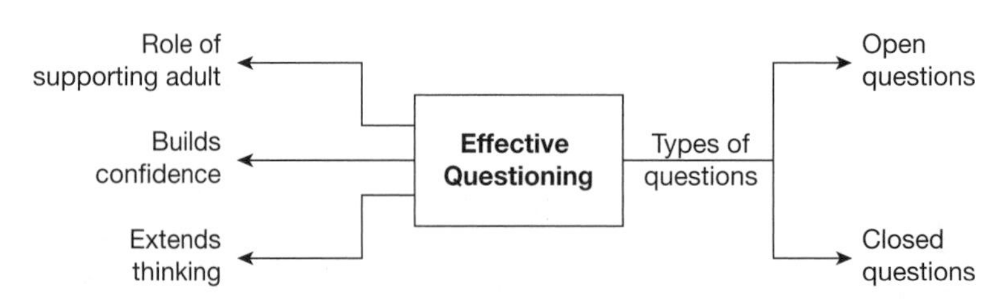

Figure 3.1 Start of a mind map

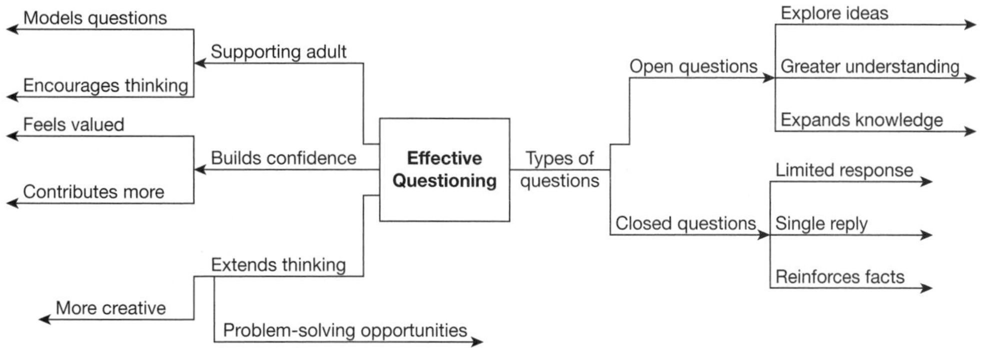

Figure 3.2 Development of mind map in Figure 3.1

One of the great advantages of a mind map is that it can allow multi-dimensional thinking, and can be expanded or contracted at any time. You can make some of the key points even more prominent by using colour or by drawing pictures. This is a useful way of going over key details after reading or listening to a lecture. You can record the key points that you are able to recall and compare these with your notes later on to see how much knowledge and understanding of the topic you have gained or forgotten!

Methods of note taking

There are several different ways of making notes, ranging from writing down ideas in a linear form to creating a mind map, but the following rules should apply to all. All notes should be:

- brief
- clear
- understandable.

You will find that different methods of note taking have different values. Find one system that suits you and stay with it, but it is a good idea to experiment a bit to begin with. Perhaps a good place to start is to look at the following methods and then see if any match your needs.

Notes made when reading text

Books and journal articles that you own can obviously be treated differently from books that are borrowed. Texts that you own can be returned to again and again, and it is not worth copying extensively from them or making too many separate notes. It can be a good idea to mark passages of interest and your own observations on the actual page of the book, but this has its drawback, as you may re-read the book looking for different meanings and be influenced by your previous markings.

You will probably devise your own system for marking text but here are a couple of ideas to consider:

- Use the end-papers of the book, or the backs of photocopies, to record your own thoughts and observations. Note down the page references for relevant sections.
- Put coloured paper markers in the book to help you return to key points – ensuring that a clue to the content is written on the paper marker that sticks out of the book so you can find it quickly later on (it helps to note the page number on the marker too, just in case it falls out of the book).

Also, mark any passages which you don't understand and write down questions as they occur to you, to investigate further at a later date.

Apply a code to the marks that you make on the text itself so that when you return to the page it is clear to you what bits were relevant, or what was unclear and needs further consideration. For example:

- Use a single line to mark an important passage.
- Use a double line to mark an important sentence that contains key ideas or that you might want to quote.
- A wavy line could be used to indicate uncertainty.
- Use arrows to connect related passages or pieces of information.

Post-it notes are also useful for marking pages or passages, and have the advantage of not falling out of the book in the same way that bits of paper might do! You can write notes or questions on the Post-its, and different coloured Post-it notes can be used as a code.

It is advisable not to use pen for notes made on a text. As your study progresses you may well wish to alter or improve your notes. Notes made in pencil can be erased and changed more easily. For the same reason, don't write in the text itself, but use the margins. It can be very difficult to re-read a text with an open mind when it is covered in notes that you have made some time ago – and probably for a different purpose.

Linear and non-linear notes

Notes made from sources other than your own books and photocopies have a *slightly* different purpose. You will need notes not only to help you to recall the central ideas and issues you have read, but also to remind you of the wider content of the text. However, it is important to remember that notes are not a substitute for texts – you should not be aiming to recreate the text in detail in your notes; rather, the notes should be sufficient to:

- remind you of the key ideas and information of the text/lecture
- direct you to any central questions or ideas that arise from your first reading
- tell you where to go to find the original source.

Once you have taken on board the idea that notes should not simply replicate the original text but should be a site of active engagement with it, the particular form of notes is not a central issue. It is useful, however, to understand the variety of ways in which the task of note taking can be approached. One major distinction exists between notes that follow the structure of the text from point A to point B and those that view the text as a whole before making connections.

The first option has been called the linear or sequential approach – because ideas and information are recorded in a line or sequence, with one following on from another. This method is closely linked to a series of assumptions about how the mind works, for example:

- Humans think and reason in the same way that they write and speak, i.e., one word or idea at a time!
- The best way to remember something is to recall it within the framework or sequence of ideas in which it was first encountered.

Educationalists and psychologists have challenged these ideas in recent years. They argue that the brain works in a non-linear, non-sequential way that can connect many ideas together at the same time. One popular method that has already been suggested is mind mapping, as advocated by Tony Buzan. You do not need to stick to these rules strictly, nor should you feel that you should always use the same method – you could combine mind mapping with a more conventional note-taking method.

HANDY HINT

Mind mapping and spider diagrams

Remember: We tend to remember things that are connected in *meaning* as well as those that are connected by *time* or *space*. Think of a London Tube map. It tells us where to get on and off, which direction and line to take, but it doesn't reflect the actual maze of tunnels that run under the city. It allows us to find our way around them without mapping them out as they really are. This is what we must do with the notes we make.

Conventional notes

Of course you don't *have* to adopt the more visual methods of Tony Buzan. More conventional forms of linear notes could be just as useful, and it is quite possible to highlight key terms within them and to indicate connecting points between ideas as they arise.

Such notes don't have to be written in long-hand and shouldn't be over-detailed. Use abbreviations and symbols and concentrate on the bones of the argument. Remember to include your own thoughts, queries and observations and to ensure that you make a distinction between your own thoughts and those of the author. Otherwise, you may return to your notes and find it difficult to distinguish between *your* ideas and what has been lifted directly from the text. Write your thoughts at the side of the page, in brackets or in a different coloured pen. Also remember to keep a careful record of the source of your material.

On the whole, you should not be copying down large chunks of text, but occasionally you will want to include the quotation of a phrase in your notes. Ensure that you distinguish directly quoted text from your own notes written in your own words, and record all the details necessary for reference later. This also applies to all forms of notes including mind maps and other diagram notes.

Consider dividing your note page into sections, for example writing notes on the left-hand side of the page and then going back and adding your own thoughts on the right-hand side. You could write in different colours, if this helps you.

And how about sharing the note taking with your group, taking turns to keep notes of a lecture and then photocopying for the rest of the group, which will give you an insight into how other students make notes and could be helpful.

HANDY HINT

Noting references

Remember that passages taken directly from a text should be marked by the use of quotation marks at the beginning and end. You *must* also note the author's name, date of publication and the page number where the quotation can be found.

You will also need the place of publication and publisher's name for the bibliography.

The chart in Figure 3.3 might be useful when taking notes; or you could design a reference sheet for yourself.

Electronic notes

If you read using a Kindle or iPad you are likely to want to take notes electronically and there are easy ways to do this using the inbuilt capabilities of the device or an app designed for the purpose. If you haven't previously taken notes electronically, then it might be worth sorting out the technology, but this can be an easy, adaptable way to keep notes when reading or attending lectures. However, the same 'rules' about keeping bibliographic details, recording your own thoughts and being able to find your notes quickly will apply.

Author:		Date of publication:
Title of book:		
Place of publication:		Publisher:
Other publication details:		
Main points including:	Pages read:	
Key words/ideas Links to other texts/authors Links to workplace practices My views Notable quotation (with page number!)		
Further links and action		

Figure 3.3 Example note-taking sheet

Taking too many notes

Lastly, it is worth remembering that if you keep over-detailed notes you are less likely to be able to sort out the key themes at a later date. Notes should be short, about keeping important, key details, about recording your thinking in response to ideas and matching ideas to other reading or to evidence from your workplace. Too much detail can obscure the view, so do not think that you have to record every detail or every word that is spoken. Keep your notes brief.

Summary

This chapter has provided an overview of the importance of taking good, accurate notes that will be of use to you at a later date. It is vital that you keep details of the books you use for study, especially of those from which you make notes. Nothing is more frustrating than having notes or quotations that you wish to use but being unable to remember from which book/e-text they originated.

Further reading

Use the study-support services available to you for additional advice: these can usually be found easily enough by visiting your institution's website or VLE (Virtual Learning Environment).

Books by the following authors contain very useful advice and guidance on note taking:

- Stella Cottrell
- Tony Buzan
- Dorothy Bedford and Elizabeth Wilson.

4 Writing academically

Introduction

The ability to write in a clear and unambiguous manner is a valuable skill in any walk of life, but especially for a student in HE, who is expected to communicate clearly some quite complex material. This chapter concentrates on some fundamental writing skills – such as paragraphing, sentence structure, punctuation and spelling rules – which should enable you to write with style and economy.

Most academics would agree with the proposition that the most important aspect of a student's writing is the accuracy and appropriateness of their ideas and arguments. Primarily, tutors and lecturers marking your work will look to see if you have understood what you were asked to do in any assignment, and how well you managed to fulfil those instructions throughout the course of your assignment. Nevertheless, it is important to remember that, in order to get your response across with accuracy and impact, you need to use the correct words in the right order. How you are understood by others will depend upon how you structure your words – if you want the academic reader to fully appreciate your ideas, you must follow some basic guidelines on how to write simply and accurately.

This chapter is only a brief introduction to the subject – many useful books are published about writing skills that may be found in your institution's library. If you suspect that you may have particular problems with writing because of dyslexia, Irlen Syndrome or another disability, then contact your institution's study support team. Such problems are surprisingly common, so you will not be alone in seeking help and often the study strategies and support will help you over the initial stages of writing as a new student and direct you to future practical help.

Writing as communication

Communication is essential if learning and teaching are to take place. As a student you will be required to convey ideas, argument and information in a variety of ways. You will be asked to communicate in the form of a written assignment, such as essays, reports, case studies or reflective journals. For this communication to be effective, it is important that you consider for whom you are writing and what they may be expecting from the assignment you have been asked to carry out.

Therefore, before you start writing, it is necessary to consider carefully the audience that you are aiming your writing at. You can do this by asking yourself some simple preparatory questions that may appear basic but are nevertheless important:

- For whom am I writing?
- What are they expecting from this piece of work?
- What am I trying to communicate to them?
- How can I best make myself understood?
- In what ways can I make my work interesting for them?
- What is the marking criterion for this piece of work?

Admittedly, this may be somewhat difficult to determine when you first begin your studies. You may be encountering new subjects, or familiar ones approached in a different way. Indeed, many students find that it takes a while before they can grasp adequately the fundamental, basic concepts and facts surrounding the topics they are attempting to learn, let alone the subtleties of appreciation and understanding shown by their lecturers and tutors.

In the midst of trying to 'get their head around' a plethora of fascinating, confusing material, students are expected to write something intelligent and meaningful about it! This can, at first, seem somewhat daunting. The good news, however, is that the people who set you your assignments were once students themselves. They appreciate that you are making the first, tentative steps on the journey towards proficiency in your studies, and do not expect perfection. Your tutors and lecturers are more likely to be interested in your willingness to attempt to understand and express your appreciation of the subject, even if you have to endure a time when your knowledge of it is somewhat limited and superficial. Additionally, as a student you also may need to work at the way in which you communicate what you have learned, refining your language skills, both orally and in writing.

Whilst it is true that reading the work of others is of great worth in helping you to develop your writing skills, it also can present hidden difficulties for the unwary.

Some students attempt to emulate in a rather crude, simplistic manner, the style of writing that they find in the textbooks that they read, simply because, to them, it sounds impressively 'academic'. Although this is perfectly understandable, unless you are careful, trying to adopt another person's writing style can produce work that lacks the immediacy and clarity of one's own mode of expression. The best approach is to try to find a 'middle road', where you retain your own unique way of thinking and expressing yourself regarding a subject, with some adjustments to make it acceptable to an academic reader.

HANDY HINT

Improving your writing through developing your reading
By far the best and most enjoyable way to gain an understanding of the rules of good expression is *to read*. Spelling, structure, style and punctuation are, very often, best appreciated and absorbed in the process of reading something which interests or challenges you.

So, try to get into *the habit* of reading for knowledge, pleasure or even diversion!

The more widely you read, whether from textbooks, e-journals or good-quality newspapers, the more aware you will become of what constitutes effective written communication. Having seen how others 'get their message across', you can use this knowledge to add interest and depth to your own writing.

Writing as self-assessment

Writing in a way that effectively communicates ideas, information and argument involves the combination of a variety of skills. In your opinion, which of the following are most important to the creation of good communicative writing?

- Writing clearly and legibly.
- Using standard forms of grammar and punctuation.
- Structuring content to provide a logical development.
- Using concrete examples from the workplace to illustrate important points.
- Choosing words carefully to create a desired effect.
- Using paragraphs to structure your answer.
- Introducing word images and metaphors to heighten meaning.

It could be argued that, to some extent, all of the above play their part in enabling a writer to convey meaning in a clear and expressive manner. But how do they relate to the creation of the *formal academic style* necessary for assignment writing in HE? Here are some pointers:

- Academic writing addresses an audience that is likely to be impressed by answers that display careful thought and reasoned argument and where statements are backed up by reliable, verifiable evidence and opinion.

- Attention should be paid to correctly observing the 'building blocks' of language, such as spelling, punctuation, sentence structure and paragraphing conventions.
- Language should not be too informal, idiomatic or colloquial. It should indicate an understanding of the terminology that is linked to the topic being studied and appropriate to discussion of the subject.

Learning which type of language and mode of expression is appropriate for your subject will take time. As you gain experience, you will become sensitive to the ways in which your tutors and authors address their topics. It is fair to say, however, that in general, academic writing is more logical, and less emotional. It relies more upon objective proof than on the kind of expression that you would find, for example, in a diary entry or in the sort of discussion you would have with friends at the pub. However, you may find that you have to use a *slightly different style depending on type of assignment* that you are asked to tackle. For example, it may be more appropriate to write in a personal, subjective manner for a reflective journal or case study than it would be for a report based upon the results of scientific enquiry or for an essay. Whatever form your written assignments may take, you will need to follow the rules of written language in order to make yourself understood.

Word and spelling strategies

Spelling words correctly is important if you do not want to distract or confuse your reader. Generally, assignments will be word-processed and this has the advantage of word/grammar checks built into the computer software. Get into the habit of checking your work regularly, but remember that the computer is a machine, and decisions will be mechanical – sometimes you will need to overrule the machine! If the spelling-checker queries a word, it might be because it is using the US dictionary, or because a word used within your studies is not recognised by the spelling-checker. You should switch to UK spellings, and enter any new words into the dictionary of the word-processing programme. Some spelling strategies are offered below that will help you to become more conscious of the ways in which English words are constructed and ordered.

Rules and patterns

Rules and patterns in English word order can help us to understand and spell words more effectively. For example, the mnemonic 'i before e, except after c' is a memorable way for determining whether to put the letter 'i' before 'e' in the middle of a word. Consider the spelling of the following words: 'p**ie**ce', 'n**ie**ce' are spelled with the '**i**' before the '**e**', whereas in 'dec**ei**ve', and 'conc**ei**ve' order of the letters is reversed because they come immediately after the letter '**c**'. Having learned such rules, you need to realise that some English words do not conform to this order and need to be learned individually, for example, 'spec**ie**s'.

This is another reason why reading critically around your subject is a valuable exercise, because it can enrich your knowledge of the intricacies of the language, helping you to observe the underlying rules of language, as well as those instances where the rules appear to be broken. It is a good idea to note down any words that you use frequently, and also note patterns or mnemonics to help you to spell correctly at those times when you are not using the word-processor.

Although a tutor assessing your work may overlook the occasional misspelling, too many mistakes will divert his/her attention from the important points you are trying to make. Misspelled work may give the impression of being sloppy and the tutor may feel that you lack a sufficiently rigorous, professional approach to the writing of your assignments. Therefore, it is well worth spending time ensuring that the words you use are spelled correctly, as well as being appropriate to the meaning you wish to convey.

HANDY HINT

Correcting words that you habitually misspell

Try to take note of any words that you habitually misspell. Keep a list of their correct spellings handy as a personal dictionary. Watch out for those that are picked up by your tutors in the feedback you receive on written assignments and make a deliberate effort to give the correct spellings in your next piece of work.

Reading your work from *right to left* (i.e. in the opposite direction to normal) can help you to identify such words, as this eliminates the sense of the passage and makes each word and its spelling stand out.

And remember, you can always use the spelling-checker on your computer to look for any errors and correct them before you hand in a piece of work. Be sure to first set the computer's spelling dictionary to English (UK) rather than English (US) spellings!

Making your own personal dictionary or glossary of terms

This can be tremendously helpful! A good-sized telephone/address book can make a particularly useful personal dictionary – you can list your new words alphabetically. Note down the correct spellings of any words that you frequently misspell, or the correct meanings of any words that you have used wrongly. Over the course of time your vocabulary will grow in terms of accuracy and sophistication, together with your understanding of your subject. If you prefer, you can keep your personal dictionary electronically.

Dictionaries and thesauruses

If you get into the habit of looking up words, you will find that the same word may have a variety of associated meanings that are dependent upon context – you can choose the meaning most appropriate to what you are trying to explain or describe.

There are also subject-specific dictionaries that will give you a breakdown of the meaning, history and usage of words and terms associated with the study of, for example, sociology or education. A starting place to find these might be in a text-book or online glossary.

Vocabulary

You will need to be precise regarding your use of words, particularly in academic writing. It is extremely easy to 'borrow' impressive-looking words and phrases from the authors you read and incorporate them into your work without understanding their specific meaning. This can have comic or tragic consequences – depending on whether you are reading the work or have written it! Many words are used incorrectly, or confused with others, for example:

- adverse and averse
- accept and except
- affect and effect
- censor and censure
- illusion and allusion.

Frequently, words that sound the same (homonyms) may be incorrectly spelled, such as:

- their (which denotes possession or belonging), e.g. *their* raincoats are wet
- there (which indicates location or place), e.g. the coats are hanging over *there*
- they're (a shortened form of ' they are'), e.g. *they're* making the floor wet.

Realistically speaking, everyone makes some errors in their use of language, particularly when essay writing is new to them. The important thing is to note these mistakes and use them positively, as a means of correcting and improving the accuracy and clarity of your writing.

Writing style

Individual subjects may have developed particular ways of thinking and expressing ideas that are specific to them. Words, ideas and arguments may be used in ways that differ from those that are appropriate for another subject. An essay, for example, may differ greatly from a case study, in the manner in which ideas are linked and ordered, in its structure and in the ways in which language is used to explain those ideas. As you listen to your tutors and lecturers or read texts on your subject, it is important to pay attention to clues regarding appropriate expression and to try to adapt your writing to these 'norms'. At the same time, do not allow your work to become so bloated with technical terms and jargon that it is difficult for a general reader to follow. Try to avoid difficult or abstract words where simple and direct ones will convey the same meaning.

Academic style

Being reflective and demonstrating critical analysis are also important elements in academic writing and will contribute to the overall academic style of writing. Of course, the tutor marking your assignment will look for your knowledge of the subject studied, but how you use that knowledge will indicate your understanding of it. Your writing should not read like a textbook, or just give information – the tutor will want to read your *interpretation* of the knowledge, and your relation of it to your own experience. Being 'critical' in this context does not mean finding fault; rather, it means looking very closely and scrutinising the knowledge that you have. This critical ability can be developed in several ways, for example, by asking yourself a range of questions that progressively probe your material:

- What is the main point I am trying to make here? What information do I have from reading to back this up?
- What expectations are raised by this knowledge, by me or by others? What would happen if ...?
- Does this change my thinking? Would it change something in the workplace? How could I find out?
- What assumptions can be drawn? Are there any inconsistencies or other opinions?

If there is a sense within your writing that you are trying to answer such questions, then you are on your way to being critically reflective – that is, demonstrating that you are searching for the meaning behind information and knowledge, connecting that meaning to your personal observations and experiences in the workplace and considering possible outcomes for the future. This will add style and weight to your writing. Usually, such analysis is threaded throughout academic work, particularly within an essay. In other academic writing formats the major part of any analysis might be contained within a single section of the writing. Such formats include case studies, reports and dissertations. However, for most assignments, an academic style of writing, in which critical analysis and reflection test relationships between ideas and practice, and query assumptions and bias, is the way to demonstrate your understanding of new (and old) knowledge.

Punctuation

Punctuation is an invaluable tool in communicating with the reader of your work. It helps to ensure that a sentence flows correctly and that words and phrases are given the stress appropriate to their meaning. Poorly punctuated prose can detract from the impact and meaning of what you are trying to express. It is therefore worthwhile spending some time to become conversant with the components of punctuation. The following are some worth revising:

The comma

The comma (,) is used to divide parts of a sentence (words, phrases and clauses) or divides items in a list. Here are some examples:

> 'The first prize, a large bouquet of flowers, was awarded to the best student.'
>
> 'The resources required to take notes in lectures include paper, coloured pens, pencils and a ruler for drawing lines.'

When writing sentences do not attempt to include too much information simply separated by commas – the meaning will be difficult to follow and the sentence is likely to break down grammatically.

The apostrophe

One use of the apostrophe is to show *possession* or *belonging*. It is important to note that the position of the apostrophe alters, depending on whether it is used with a noun in its *singular* form (before the 's') or *plural* form (after the 's'). For example:

Singular	**Plural**
Julie's arm	The little boys' room
The man's coat	The teachers' union
A dog's life	The nurses' coats

An apostrophe is also used to indicate *the omission of letters in a word*. In everyday speech, words are often abbreviated. For example:

don't = do not
can't = can not
you'll = you will.

It is worth noting that such contractions, where words have been abbreviated, are rarely acceptable in academic writing. It is better to give the full spelling of the word, unless you are trying to convey spoken dialogue or vernacular language.

Care should be taken not to confuse 'its' (meaning 'belonging to it') with 'it's' (meaning 'it is'). In most cases 'its' does not require an apostrophe!

The colon

The colon (:) indicates a connection between two parts of a sentence, where the second part explains or expands upon the first part. For example:

> The lesson dragged on: punctuation was a difficult topic.

A colon should also be used to indicate a balance between the meaning of the first and second parts of the sentence. For example:

> He loved to perform: his audiences adored him.

Commonly, colons are used in a sentence to introduce a list of items. For example:

> Authors writing about aspects of child development include: Mary Sheridan, Carolyn Meggitt, Malcolm Hughes and Laura E. Berk.

Finally, colons are used to *introduce quotations*. For example:

> Greedy (2013 p. 4) writes: 'Chocolate really helps to encourage study.'

The quotation mark

Quotation marks (' ') and (" ") are indispensable, as students will frequently need to quote from an author's work in their written assignments. Double quotation marks or 'speech marks' are, by convention, put around speech. For example:

> "My goodness, these cakes are delicious", commented Mary.

However, when quoting *from a text* it is appropriate to use single quotation marks.

> As Meggitt (2012, p. 3) observes: 'Moral and spiritual development consists of a maturing awareness of how to relate to others ethically, morally and humanely.'

Single quotation marks are also used to indicate that a word or phrase that is being used has been taken from somewhere (or someone) else. For example:

> The American Revolution was led by 'sons of freedom'.

Units of expression

There are two main groupings of material within a piece of writing, namely, sentences and paragraphs.

Sentences

Essentially, sentences are series of words grouped together in a meaningful manner. Each sentence should contain one central idea and must conform to certain grammatical rules. It must imply a subject and predicate (or, to put it differently, subject, verb and object). Take the following sentence as an example:

The maddened bull ran straight towards the china shop.

The *subject* of this sentence, the main focus of attention, is the bull, which happens to be the main 'doer' in this scene. The *verb* or 'doing word' in this sentence is 'ran', and tells us what action is taking place. Finally, the *object* of this sentence, both grammatically and literally, is the china shop – and tells us more about the nature of the action. Without all three of these components in place, the sentence would fail to clearly communicate its meaning to the reader and we would have to guess at its significance.

Of course, sentences can be much more complex than the example given above and have more than one subject, verb or object. However, the main things to bear in mind when writing a sentence is that it should aim to convey *one controlling idea* and should make sense on its own. Consider the following: 'With all the taps running.' It should be obvious that this is not a complete sentence, because it does not make sense on its own or make a clear statement of the facts. With the provision of a little more information, the statement is complete and we have a fully functioning sentence: 'The forgetful child left the bathroom with all the taps running.'

HANDY HINT

Checking that your sentences are correct

One way of ensuring that your sentences are complete is to read them out to someone else or to record them and listen to what you have written. If the meaning is difficult to ascertain, then your sentences most probably need some adjustment to make them 'whole'.

Breaking up very long sentences into a number of shorter ones can help you to get your message across. Also, using more straightforward terms (rather than difficult words and expressions that you do not fully understand) can add directness and clarity to your writing. There may be occasions, however, where you have to include technical terms that have no other appropriate or satisfactory alternative.

Paragraphs

Paragraphs are groupings of sentences on a common theme. As such, they serve to indicate to your reader the starting and finishing place of a given topic, idea or stage in your argument. Properly used, they can help to give order and structure to your written expression.

Each new paragraph should open with a *topic sentence.* This is a sentence that introduces or encapsulates the main idea that the paragraph will develop. Following sentences will then elaborate on or explain this main topic. The final sentence(s) of the paragraph will summarise the most important points and issues raised around that topic and perhaps lead (link) into the next idea or topic to be introduced.

Try to avoid making your paragraphs exhaustively long (e.g. by attempting to introduce too many main points within a single passage) or too short (e.g. by raising a point without any attempt to explore or develop it). Never rely on 'one-sentence paragraphs' to get your meaning across, because one-sentence paragraphs are limited to information only, and rarely contain any reflection or analysis. The guiding principle here is that the paragraph should be long enough for you to adequately express the ideas while still maintaining the reader's interest.

The benefits of correctly structured sentences and paragraphs cannot be emphasised too strongly. The order of words on a page has a dramatic effect on the ability of those words to convey the meaning that you hope to communicate. By taking time to apply some of these simple rules you can add tremendous force and clarity to your written assignments. When you next read a piece of writing that impresses or moves you, look to see how the writer has made use of these simple but vital guiding principles of effective writing. Then, consider how you can 'stand on the shoulders' of these experts by incorporating and adapting these elements of effective communication into your own writing.

Summary

This chapter has emphasised the importance of learning some of the 'ground rules' of written expression, such as how to structure and punctuate sentences and how to develop a vocabulary that is appropriate to the subject about which you are writing.

As with the acquisition of other skills in life, learning to write clearly and succinctly does not happen overnight – it necessarily involves practice, as well as taking chances and making mistakes, and trying to find a written style that suits both yourself and your reader. Learning to write for an academic audience can be likened to a baby learning to walk. As you move forward, you learn and try out new rules, see if you have achieved the right balance and make adjustments for the next step. Eventually, as you continue, the fear of falling is overtaken by the exhilaration of being able to move forward with increasing independence and agility. The main thing is to persevere – take 'baby' steps until your writing eventually 'finds its feet'.

Further reading

Make the most of the resources available to you from your institution's study support services. There is a great deal of advice available on the internet, but do be very careful about which sources you use. Generally, those from universities are suitable. A couple of other websites that you may find helpful for writing are:

www.literacytrust.org
www.englishgrammar.org.

In addition to these resources, try searching for the following authors' books, all of which contain very useful advice and guidance on themes discussed in this chapter:

Stella Cottrell
Dr John Peck and Martin Coyle Ann Raimes
Derek Soles
Lynne Truss
Kathi Wyldeck.

Reference

Meggitt, C. (2012) *Child Development: an illustrated guide with DVD (3rd edn).* Essex: Pearson Educational Limited.

5 Planning and writing essay-type assignments

Introduction

This chapter will consider the skills needed to produce academic writing assignments of various kinds based upon essay structure. It will consider the reasoning behind the academic discipline of writing, and also the *preparation* and *writing* of academic work.

The preparation for essay writing is often overlooked by students, so the first section of the chapter focuses on the work that is involved in *preparing* an essay or piece of writing: *planning* and *gathering material* together for your assignment. You may feel under pressure to get something down on paper before you have had the chance to fully properly appreciate what you are attempting to achieve. In fact, the success of a piece of writing often depends as much on how you have organised and interpreted the material as the way in which you have written it. The second section deals with the structure and organisation of the essay. It introduces ways to reflect upon the style of academic work and includes discussion of narrative versus critical styles of writing and the use of evidence to support an argument.

Most HE courses require students to produce written assignments of some description as part of their coursework; answering examination questions also involves basic essay-writing skills. So, mastery of such skills is essential to your success and you will need to make time to *think*, *plan* and *practise* the art of assignment writing. Feedback from your marking tutor after each assignment – however painful the comments – can be used constructively to improve your approach and performance next time. Making mistakes and learning from them is an important part of the whole learning process.

Why write essays and assignments?

Essays and written assignments are set by your tutors for a variety of reasons. Consider some of the most important:

- Essays and written assignments make you *think* about the material studied; writing an assignment requires you to look back over your coursework, notes made and the lectures you have attended. Rather than the material remaining as a pool of *potential* knowledge, writing an essay or assignment enables you to *activate* this information. By attempting to make sense of this material, structuring it to address a specific question, you transform it into *actual*, transferable knowledge and understanding. This requires you to *discriminate*, to be *selective*, prioritising and reshaping some ideas and information and rejecting others. So, having to write something on a topic encourages you to make an attempt to *understand* it and *apply* your knowledge and judgement regarding it – which otherwise might not happen.
- Writing on a subject should stimulate you to consider what *your own views* are regarding it and to express those views in a coherent, persuasive manner. In other words, you are forced to think about what your own *position* is on certain subjects and about the sorts of critical and evaluative judgements required to support your point of view. However, it is also important to include evidence, from reading and personal experience, that supports your view.
- Essays and written assignments comprise one of the ways that your tutors can *assess your progress* and identify areas of particular strength and weakness in your work.
- Writing assignments *enhances your writing style*. They help you to think and express yourself in a disciplined, accurate and precise manner.
- Essays are good practice for other activities that involve organising and conveying information, such as examinations and oral presentations. This extends into professional life in the workplace, where, although they are not academically assessed, written forms of communication are commonplace.

The nature of the essay/assignment

Writing assignments have many benefits, in terms of the development of valuable skills. To some extent, having to commit pen to paper or fingers to keyboard is a worrisome task. Many students envisage that, in writing something that other people will read and judge, they have to create a word-perfect piece of work.

Certainly, you should try to make a piece of writing as accurate as possible and not just a copy of what has been read elsewhere. On the other hand, it is worth bearing in mind that the word *essay* derives from the French verb 'essayer', which means 'to try' or 'to attempt'. Tutors are *not* expecting perfection from your writing.

Rather, they are looking to see that you are *attempting* to understand an issue and *trying* to say something relevant, meaningful and true about it, in your own particular way.

Problems with essay writing

Before we outline the skills necessary for successful academic writing, we will pause briefly and look at some of the most common difficulties that arise with students' writing. Stop and consider if any of these comments might apply to your own writing and what you would do to rectify them.

- *Failure to interpret the essay title or understand the assignment brief.* Frequently, students misinterpret the basic nature or purpose of the assignment itself. There are a number of reasons for this, but chief amongst them is a basic misunderstanding of key words such as 'discuss', critique' or 'compare' in the essay title or instructions. These words have quite specific meanings, so you will need to ensure that you understand what such instructions mean by looking them up in a dictionary or discussing them with your tutor. Perhaps the assignment requires you to carry out a number of related but separate activities and present findings in different ways – this may confuse you and you will need to check it out. Don't be afraid to ask your tutors to help you to clarify any terms or instructions that you find difficult to follow, or the particular emphasis that you should give to the various parts of an assignment. Tutors much prefer to do this at the initial stage, rather than to find out later, after the assignment has been handed in for marking, that you did not fully understand what the assignment was asking you to do.
- *Too descriptive writing/writing lacking in critical analysis.* This comment arises when an essay presents information (usually too much of it) but makes no attempt to *evaluate* the significance or meaning of the information. It is not enough to tell your reader *what* the facts are, you also need to indicate *why* you have introduced them and *how* they support the case you are making, i.e. your *interpretation* of these facts.
- *Lack of supporting evidence.* This is almost the reverse situation, where a position is taken on an issue and arguments and assertions are made without providing any *back-up* for them. A student may claim or express a particular opinion in an essay without providing any *evidence* to corroborate his/her statement. Such unsupported claims are normally regarded as being incompatible with academic writing – cogent reasons should be given as to why a particular view has been put forward.
- *Lack of structure/incoherence.* If too little time and thought have been given to planning the way in which you intend to answer a question, the result is very often an essay that lacks structure, order and logical development. Such essays

tend to stagger from point to point in a rather random manner, failing to adequately address the key issues or to come to a satisfying conclusion. A written assignment is rather like a plant that needs a lot of pruning and shaping before it can show its inherent structural beauty, i.e. you may need to reorder and reorganise the parts of your essay a number of times before your argument flows in a way that best develops the ideas you are trying to put forward.

Having taken a cautionary look at some of the pitfalls associated with written assignments, you are now well placed to consider some ways in which to avoid them in your writing.

Approaching the essay question

Your starting point is the essay title or the assignment instructions. These establish the boundaries of the material that you should cover in your essay and give vital details regarding how you should approach it. If you are given assignment instructions, rather than an essay title, use them to create a 'working title' for your assignment. Try to sum up, in one or two sentences, what the assignment is asking you to do, as this will help you to focus and structure your answer.

Different questions require different answers. For example:

> Discuss: 'Revision of the Primary National Curriculum 2013: enabling tool or restrictive practice?'

or

> Describe how the revision of the Primary National Curriculum for 2013 creates an effective educational framework for learning.

Both assignments cover the same area of information (Primary National Curriculum), but each one actually requires a subtly different response. The first question asks you to 'discuss' or *weigh up* and *define* the National Curriculum document, to make *critical judgements* regarding whether it should be considered as having an enhancing or limiting influence on pupils' learning. (Of course, the answer is likely to be somewhere between these two 'poles' and will require you to carefully balance the pros and cons of both positions before you arrive at a considered answer.)

The second question requires you to 'describe' this initiative. Quite obviously, this will involve rather more *description* of the National Curriculum than does the first example. However, although it is not explicitly stated in the essay title, the answer will also require you to provide further *definition* and *analysis* regarding *how* the National Curriculum revision is likely, based on your reading of the evidence, to assist the learning process. As in the first question, you will also probably need to make judgements regarding how and to what extent the revision assists or otherwise. In this instance, however, your answer will be focused specifically on whether or not it provides an effective learning framework, and will involve a consideration of the 'scaffolding' appropriate to effective learning. So, although the questions are similar, the responses appropriate to each are different, in that the focus of attention is directed at a slightly different aspect of the revised National Curriculum and its effect on learning.

So, how do you know what is being asked of you in any given assignment? A crucial step is to separate out:

a) The *content* words, which indicate what kind of factual material needs to be covered by the assignment

b) The *procedure* words, which tell you how to *handle* this content, such as 'discuss', 'analyse' and so on (Figure 5.1).

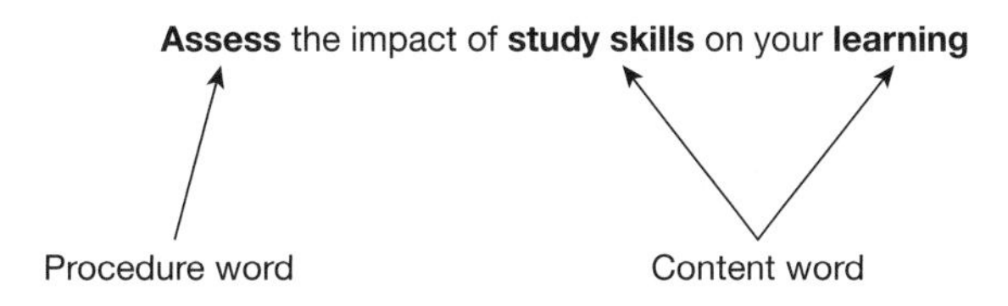

Figure 5.1 Analysing an essay assignment

Whenever you are given an essay title or assignment instructions, make a point of underlining or highlighting these essential bits of information and giving them some considered thought. Identifying these key terms should give you an initial idea of what material needs to be covered by your assignment and the perspective from which you should view it.

Although some questions may use terms that appear to be deliberately vague or provocative, almost all will require you to find a *suitable definition* before you can begin to answer the question. For example:

> There is no such thing as 'special needs'. Discuss.

In order to answer a question of this kind one would have to begin by considering what is meant by the term 'special needs'. Is it best understood in a historical, economic, sociological, political or personal sense? Your decision will, of course, be influenced by the area you are studying. For example, if your academic discipline is early childhood studies, this will shape your definition of this key term and the direction from which you will approach the question.

Another assignment example might be:

> Produce a written essay of 1500 words reflecting on how national policies impact on children's learning and learning behaviour.

Here, you will need to be clear about what is meant by 'learning and learning behaviour'. Your definition of this term would determine, to a large extent, the nature of your answer, although of course you would need to match this with your knowledge of the *impact* of national policies. This in itself might be a challenge, as you would need to determine which national policies were relevant and appropriate – although your course of study should provide an answer to this query.

In most assignments *definition of terms* is necessary in order to inform your reader, *from the outset*, how you have understood and interpreted the question that was set.

To sum up, essay and assignment questions, whatever the subject area, are constructed in a way that is intended to give you 'clues' about how to provide an appropriate answer; clues regarding content, approach and the sort of response that is required from you, the writer. Take time to look for those clues, discuss them with your colleagues, friends and family. And remember, you can always go back to your tutor to confirm if you are 'on the right lines' before you embark on lots of time-consuming research.

Expectations of your essay/assignment

Before moving on to the business of gathering material for your essay, pause briefly to consider what your tutors *may expect* from your writing and what you should be working towards when interpreting questions, re-reading notes and planning your work. Below is a brief list of some of the most important qualities that tutors expect to find when reading an academic essay. Try to ensure that you build these components into your essays.

- *Relevance to the topic.* Has your answer focused on the areas required? Have you considered the topic in sufficient depth and detail? Have you shown familiarity with key terms, theories, players and events that are central to the topic you are exploring?

- *Use of appropriate sources.* Does your work reflect sufficient breadth and depth of reading from valid and appropriate sources of information? Does the assignment require you to use *primary* (first-hand) source materials, *secondary* sources (from books and articles written on a topic) or *both*? How have you used the source material that you have gathered? Have you made an attempt to weigh it up, assessing its importance and relevance, verifying its truthfulness through critical analysis?

HANDY HINT

Ensuring critical content/analysis in your assignments

It is very easy and tempting to cram your assignment full of facts, examples and references taken from your reading. However, these will be of very little value to your essay unless you make an attempt to let your reader know *why* you have included them.

If you introduce a topic or raise an issue, you will need to explore it, assess its worth and integrate it into your overall argument or treatment of the subject.

HANDY HINT

A list of 'who did what', 'who said what' or 'what happened next' is all well and good, but what do these things prove or *mean*? How do they help to *develop* the case you are putting forward?

Your tutors will expect to see this *evaluation* and *analysis* at various points throughout your essay.

- *Argument and organisation*. Your assignment should present a reasoned and coherent argument to your reader. The material should be arranged in a logical manner, around clearly defined points. You should provide evidence, in the form of observations from the workplace and facts taken from reliable sources or expert opinion, in support of these points, together with an appreciation of alternative points of view.

HANDY HINT

What is academic argument?

In this context, an 'argument' is not necessarily a disagreement but, rather, the presentation of evidence that proves a point.

It is possible to give a balanced view of an argument, giving evidence from two sides or even more. Just imagine two politicians presenting different views on education!

In your essay, you need to present your own argument, your own views – but with evidence from reading and the workplace to back up your argument. However, it is good practice to acknowledge that there are other ways of interpreting the evidence and that others may hold different opinions. This shows that you understand the limitations of your work and can appreciate that not everyone sees things in the same way!

- *Presentation*. The standard of presentation of your work, to some extent, affects the way in which it is perceived by the person marking it. Communication between writer and reader is enhanced greatly if a piece of work is neatly laid out, grammatically correct, legible and well structured. Sloppy presentation can give the impression that your ideas may also be untidy and formed without due care and attention. Some departments provide quite detailed instructions regarding the layout of written assignments, specifying such things as line spacing, margin size, the type and size of font to use and the manner in which to reference your sources of information. It is wise to follow such instructions, as they assist you in presenting your work in the best possible format.

HANDY HINT

Ensuring an appropriate format for your written work
Try to allow yourself time to 'tidy up' the presentation of your written work. Follow closely any guidelines your department may provide regarding the layout of your script. These may include:

- How you identify your piece of work – are you allowed to place your name on your script, or do you have to use an ID code.
- Check appropriate font type and size, line and paragraph spacing, width of margins, references and bibliographies, numbering of pages and word count, or even the kind of folder or binding to use when submitting work.

Paying attention to such details prepares the way for your work to be seen in a favourable light by the person grading your assignment. In addition, learning and applying these rules not only helps to structure your answer but, in the long run, also sets you free to concentrate on the more creative, satisfying aspects of academic writing.

Gathering materials

Having thought about your essay/assignment question, you will then begin the process of weaving together materials from which you will craft your answer. This tends to be the most time-consuming aspect of academic writing but can also be the most rewarding. Preparing materials requires you to be *selective* and to decide which of the things you have read are most *significant* and *relevant.* Individuals tackle this activity in different ways, but here is one suggested approach:

- *Identify the topic area.* Carefully and deliberately consider what the essay question/ assignment brief is *specifically* asking you to do. Many students rush this stage, wasting precious days and even weeks reading through material in the hope that *something* they will read will *somehow* help them answer the question. A far better strategy is to first *meditate* on exactly which aspect of a particular topic the essay is asking you to address. Such quiet reflection clarifies the task in hand. This should enable you to 'get into the mind' of the person who set the assignment, figuring out *why* you have been set this assignment, what are likely to be the *most important* issues surrounding it, and what sorts of arguments and evidence are likely to be most compelling. By doing so you should be well on your way to knowing what kinds of information to look for in your reading.

  At this very open, 'fluid' stage a concept (mind) map or spider diagram may be useful in helping you to arrange your ideas. Rough outline notes can also serve the purpose of helping you to construct *possible* arrangements of material for an answer. Consider what *slant* you are going to give to the essay. Write a set of questions to help guide your research and look for the answers to these questions. Begin to consider the specific *search terms* (words, phrases, authors) that you will need to use in order to locate material in the library or on the internet (see Chapter 8 for more on search strategies). Have any books on the subject been *recommended* by tutors during lectures or on reading lists? These may indicate the major critical debates that have taken place regarding this topic/subject.

- *Re-read your notes.* Make notes from your reading that focus specifically on the issues raised by the assignment. Decide which material is strictly relevant and which material you can afford to reject. As you read, keep asking yourself: 'Do I need this information and, if I do, how will I use it?'
- *Where necessary, add to your material.* This may include further reading, checking facts or ensuring that you have reference (publication) details for texts that you wish to use. Finding useful quotations or evidence in support of your position is also part of this stage. Finally, if your source material is quite old, you may need to see what has been written on the subject more recently, particularly if you are considering issues of a topical nature or that have contemporary applications.

There are a range of difficulties to be aware of at this stage of the essay-writing process. The first arises from not giving yourself enough time to read as widely as you need in order to give a comprehensive answer to the set question. This usually leads to essays that are quite superficial, and repetitive. The second occurs when you give too much time to reading and not enough to analysing the material you have read and gathered. Too much information can become unmanageable and can obscure the focus of the essay itself.

When composing an essay, try to envisage each section of your answer as being a mini-essay in itself, requiring you to: introduce a new idea, develop and support it and conclude by indicating how it helps to answer a central theme of the essay question itself. Doing this should ensure that you ask the right questions of the books, articles and other source materials you are reading and making notes from, at each stage of your answer. Here are some useful questions to ask as you read and make notes:

- Does this reading relate to an important aspect of the topic I am writing on?
- How does it fit in with the information I have gathered already?
- Does it cover something new, or is it the same material worded differently?
- How can I use this material to support my argument(s) in this essay?
- What are the implications that arise from introducing this material and how should I interpret and develop these ideas in my assignment?

HANDY HINT

Ensuring that your descriptions include meaningful reflection

If your writing is centred on some research or task that you have carried out, ensure that your writing *reflects* your reading and study and is not just a *description* of what you have done!

Remember, tutors probably already know much of the information that you are encountering for the first time. What they are evaluating is *what you have made* of that material; that is, the ideas and insights you produce as a result of *reflecting* on, *weighing up* and *making sense of* what you have read or experienced.

Planning your essay or assignment writing

Once you have gathered your material and thought about how to approach the essay question, you are more than half way through. The next stage is to *plan*. Planning is essential, and should never be overlooked: without a clearly thought-out structure or framework your writing is likely to wander and it is quite likely that both you and your reader will soon get lost. Planning enables you to establish a skeleton on which to support the body of your essay/assignment and makes it much more likely that you will keep to the point.

Whether you record your ideas in a non-linear (e.g. mind map – see Chapter 3) or linear manner, you will need to give some priority and sequence to the ideas and supporting material that you have noted down. Writing itself is a linear process, so work out the sequence before you start to write. If you are using a graphical system, such as a spider diagram, where you note your ideas spatially around central topics, you will need to group related material together, perhaps using arrows, numbers or colours, so that the entries on your visual plan are connected together under main arguments and supporting points. Then you need to decide which argument comes first, which follows it and so on. If you are planning in a linear manner (perhaps making a list or arranging your notes), group the information under headings and sub-headings.

Identify the connections between the different pieces of information that you have collected, and how they relate to the main argument in your essay. Make a note of any insights that you have, even if you don't know where they might fit in at this stage. Somewhere down the line you may find the space where this piece of the jigsaw fits perfectly and helps to complete the design of your essay.

HANDY HINT

Avoiding a 'model answer' mentality in writing

Don't worry if things appear a little disordered and 'out of control' at this stage. Manipulating ideas requires a degree of 'playful creativity', which can, at first, seem unnerving. In reality, the same question can be answered with success in a variety of ways.

HANDY HINT

Academics are aware of this and usually do not have a fixed idea of a 'model' answer. Indeed, it is quite refreshing when a student finds a different and innovative approach to answering a frequently addressed topic – as long as their argument and evidence is sound and persuasive.

To sum up, a plan will allow you to play around with the order in which you might present your materials. As this plan develops you should be able to number the stages in your argument and tie together the various parts of your answer. However you work, a plan is a logical step towards success.

Your essay should have a beginning, middle and end and your plan should eventually reflect this logical sequence. However, it is important to remember that your essay plan or mind map serves two main functions. The first is to enable you to *play around creatively* with your ideas, looking for possible connections between the materials you have gathered and suggest possible ways to address the essay question. Secondly, the plan should then enable you to *organise* your ideas and information in a rather more disciplined way, so that they form a coherent, unfolding argument, analysis or narrative. Careful planning will provide greater freedom and order to your essay answer.

HANDY HINT

Ensuring that you spend an appropriate amount of time/words on any section of a written assignment

Some students, after deciding on how many topics or main ideas to introduce, will divide up the word count for the essay accordingly. Knowing roughly the maximum number of words they can write on each theme provides a guide to how much time and effort they can afford to spend on researching and writing each section.

If you have followed these guidelines your essay plan should:

- be ordered
- be legible
- address the essay question or assignment details
- include an introductory and a concluding stage
- show the development of your thinking
- include examples to support ideas and arguments, e.g. work-based tasks
- show the stages of your argument

- show connections between stages, e.g. how one idea leads to another
- identify your ideas and those that you have taken from elsewhere.

The planning grid at the end of Chapter 6 may help you with this process.

Writing: structure and content

Having completed the planning stage of your assignment and gathered the necessary information, you are now well placed to begin writing up your findings. At this stage in the writing process you should have a clear idea of:

- What the essay question/assignment is asking you to do
- How you will respond, that is, the approach you will take
- What arguments, workplace and other evidence and information you will use
- How you intend to structure and order that material.

Having determined, to some extent at least, the overall shape of your answer, you can be relatively confident that you will be providing a reasonable response to the essay or assignment brief. Next comes the somewhat fraught business of committing words to paper and beginning to find an appropriate way of 'giving birth' to those ideas through your own particular means of expression.

The following sections look at some important issues to consider when writing up an essay or assignment:

- Introductions and conclusions
- Narrative and analysis
- Use of evidence, illustration and argument
- Avoiding plagiarism.

Introduction, main body and conclusion

In everyday life we are very aware that the first impression we make when meeting another person has a strong influence on their perception of us. If we make a bad impression, for whatever reason, it takes a lot of hard work for us to convince them they were wrong. The same principle applies to written assignments, where the 'unseen' reader of our piece of communication needs to be convinced of the 'suitability' of our writing, often at quite an early stage. *Introductions* in written assignments perform the function of creating a suitable interface between writer and reader, of bringing one mind into harmony with another. Perhaps the best way of achieving this speedily is to give your reader a clear, unambiguous statement of your aims. So, at its most basic level, an introduction lets your reader know:

- *what* you intend to write about
- *why* you are tackling the subject under consideration in a particular way
- *what* you hope to achieve by the end of the essay.

By making your aims and objectives clear at the outset, you let your reader know what to expect from your assignment in terms of content, and also where you are coming from critically. Rather like a trailer advertising a feature film, your introduction will make the first important step in helping your reader to appreciate your work, because it will have set the scene, intellectually, for an understanding of your subject. Because essays and other written assignments are attempting to convey quite sophisticated ideas in a relatively small number of words, introductions need to be kept brief. Usually the introduction is no more than 10 per cent of the word count for the whole essay, which normally translates into one or two paragraphs at most.

The introductory text should describe in general terms what the essay is attempting to do, i.e. your main aim. The focus needs to be broad enough for your reader to see your overall purpose and the context of your answer. So, if, for example, you are trying to determine the most effective methods of communicating scientific principles in a science lesson, it is important to let your reader know this explicitly and simply – do not attempt to introduce too much detail at this early stage, as this might hinder the reader's ability to identify your aims. The function of the introduction is to lay out the overall dimensions or scope of your essay.

Following on from this, you may wish to outline your objectives: the individual stages of your argument or the issues that you intend to address. Here is an example of an introduction to an assignment looking at the way children learn science in the primary classroom:

> In examining this topic the essay will firstly examine common methods of introducing science in the primary classroom, taking examples from School A. Secondly, the author will compare and contrast these with the findings of recent research by E and F into principles of scientific communication. Finally, the essay will argue that, while traditional methods of learning science may have a number of advantages in certain areas, these are outweighed by the interactive opportunities offered by technological innovation.

As you can see from this example, the intention is not to spell out the entire argument in detail but to 'whet the appetite' of the reader by highlighting the main questions and/or the main concerns that the essay will be addressing. In other words, the introduction is a major signpost, letting the reader know the distance and direction of the journey they are about to undertake.

The *main body* of the essay is where you set out the substance of your argument in detail. In this section you will need to cover each of the main topics or components of your answer. Each topic or stage in the development of your argument will be covered in one or more paragraphs, depending on the importance of the material. Each main point needs to be ordered in a logical sequence – chronologically, theoretically or logically – depending on your treatment of the subject. Each section needs to be linked to the next, so that you can show your reader how one part follows on from another; this also helps to address the essay question itself.

Finally, you should aim to make a lasting impression on your reader in the *conclusion*. As in the introduction, the conclusion should be an overview or summing up of the essay's content, not an exhaustively detailed account, and so, again, you would not ordinarily use more than 10 per cent of the word count. You will need to briefly summarise the overall argument and the main themes that have been covered, condensing the evidence and how you have interpreted it. However, your main focus here will be to state clearly what conclusions your study has reached. Your reader will be keen to know not only what your findings are, but also why you consider them to be important or significant.

You may also be able to suggest some possible implications of your conclusions and even make some recommendations for future research or practice. In your last couple of sentences, recap your argument very briefly, linking it to the essay title or assignment brief so as to show how you have answered, or attempted to answer, the question that was set. Do not introduce any new information at this stage – there will not be any opportunity to develop it, and it would detract from the force of your summation.

HANDY HINT

Writing striking introductions and conclusions

As introductions and conclusions make such a strong impression on a reader, it is best to spend some extra time getting them right. Very often it is only after you have finished writing your essay that you have an accurate idea of the shape and content of your answer. So, it makes sense to go back over your introduction, making any necessary adjustments, so that what you say you are *going to do* reflects what your essay has *actually done*.

It is also useful to leave your reader with something that is memorable and that encapsulates the most important insights you have gained from your study. A suitably chosen *quotation* can do this, adding a measure of gravity and impact to the conclusions you have reached in your assignment. Or, you can point the way forward to future action or future trends.

Conclusions are the places where you round up and emphasise the central arguments or initiatives of your essay or assignment. Conclusions are where you highlight problematic areas, pose questions that still need answering or point out research that needs to be pursued.

Essay structure checklist

The following checklist may help you to ensure that your essay has an appropriate academic structure:

- Title/essay question
  - If I have been given a title, have I included it and ensured that my essay has attempted to answer its central question?
- Introduction
  - Have I shown the reader, in general terms, how I have understood what the question is asking me to do?
  - Have I then told the reader how I intend to divide up the topic, addressing the major issues that I hope to develop in the essay?
  - Have I suggested the methodology that I will use, such as the order in which I will present each subdivision, and how I will address each issue?
- Main body
  - Has/have my first paragraph(s) tackled the first issue identified in my Introduction?
  - Has it begun with a topic sentence that summarises what the section intends to do?
  - Do the following sentences aid in exploring and developing that idea?
  - Do they provide sufficient description, explanation, analysis and reference material, so that my argument in this section has been backed up sufficiently?
  - Is it clear how this section helps to provide part of an answer to the essay question itself? Have I attempted to show how this section links into the one that follows it?
  - Does each following paragraph/section have these essential components, as above, and can each be read as a 'mini-essay', introducing, developing and concluding one major aspect of the essay's answer?
- Conclusion
  - Does my conclusion summarise the overall argument and main stages of my essay?
  - Does it clearly indicate the position I have finally reached as an answer to the essay question?
  - Have I shown the reader what I consider to be the most significant aspect of this enquiry for me, the writer?
- Bibliography
  - Have I listed all of the sources of information I have used to compile this essay, following the rules of the referencing system advocated by my department?

Narrative versus critical analysis

A very frequent comment by tutors regarding students' essays is that the work consists of rather too much narrative (description) and relatively too little in the way of reflection, analysis or 'critical analysis'.

What is narrative?

Essentially, narrative is a description or an account of something. Typically, it is the relating of a list of facts and events that have some connection, such as:

> Children first learn speech patterns from their parents or caregivers, starting with gurgles and chuckles and then developing sounds, words and finally sentences.

Of course, narrative can be more complex than this. The important thing to note is that for most written assignments such narrative is simply the starting point for a discussion of these facts. Essentially, tutors are looking for argument, debate, evaluation and commentary. The detail or narrative is there to support these aspects of your analysis of the material, showing that you appreciate the significance of the facts you relate.

That is not to say that narrative and description do not have an important part to play in your essay – they set the scene and connect and make clear the ideas you are trying to communicate – but they do not form the main substance of your essay. They should support your argument or analysis.

What is analysis/critical analysis?

Essentially, analysis denotes an academic way of thinking and involves:

- weighing up evidence
- thinking critically and/or objectively about terms and explanations
- giving explanations that fit the evidence
- seeing connections between ideas and facts
- expressing your own ideas and opinions
- interpreting information to find its significance
- arguing for some ideas and against others.

Essentially, critical analysis consists of the answers to persistent, pertinent questioning of the evidence that you have gathered and opinion that you have formed in respect to any particular question or problem. It is the result of a detective-like approach; when you weigh up the significance and validity of any given piece of information in connection with your chosen topic, the resulting evaluation will include critical analysis. Such 'questions' and their answers should guide your writing but do not pose the questions in your essay itself, as you might be expected to fully answer them and this might provide too much of a challenge!

Evidence of critical analysis in your work is considered to be important because it demonstrates that you have attempted to understand and make sense of the raw material that you have studied. In essence, it indicates a search for 'wisdom' or expertise in your chosen discipline, rather than a mere accumulation of knowledge.

Evidence, illustration and argument

Another common problem is that very often a student will fail to *prove* the points that they have made. An essay full of general statements and personal own points of view is of no interest unless it contains the concrete detail necessary to substantiate them. The use of both evidence and illustrative detail is essential if you are to convince your reader of your argument or analysis.

Evidence includes any material that establishes something as a fact or clearly lends credence to a particular viewpoint. For example, an assignment may require you to provide statistical evidence, material taken from official statements made by the government or professional bodies or even photographic and film evidence. Simply, evidence can be taken from any relevant, reliable source appropriate to your subject that helps you to prove the claims that you make in your writing.

Illustration, on the other hand, is material that *lends weight to* or *helps to define* your own ideas and interpretations but does *not* necessarily prove them. For example, you may choose to draw on the opinions of a recognised expert in your field of study so as to add authority to the view that you are proposing. Or you may introduce an observation that you have made in the workplace or classroom to support a particular point of view. Although your example does not *prove* that you are correct, it is nevertheless very useful in that it does suggest to your reader that there are things in favour of the case you are making.

HANDY HINT

Ensuring a balanced consideration of evidence/opinion in an essay
In some assignments you will be required to weigh up the evidence, argument and opinion on both sides of a particular issue. Don't be put off if you find a number of equally recognised 'experts' who have very differing positions, sometimes based on the same evidence.

It is simply your job to try to weigh the opinion and evidence of one against the other and suggest which you tend to agree with on certain points, and why. However, don't forget to give your reader specific examples of such evidence and opinion for and against a particular point, and tell your reader *what these suggest to you.*

When including evidence and illustration in your assignment it will be necessary for you to indicate the sources of that material, i.e. you will have to reference it (see Chapter 6 for information about Harvard-style referencing). It is appropriate here to mention an important issue related to referencing – the implication that someone else's work is your own, otherwise known as *plagiarism*.

Avoiding plagiarism

The verb 'to plagiarise' comes from the Latin *plagiarius*, which means, literally, 'kidnapper'. So, to plagiarise is to take something that was given birth to by someone else and steal away with it, calling it your own! A more prosaic definition is provided by the Concise Oxford Dictionary (10th edition), which states that to plagiarise is to 'take (the work or an idea of someone else) and pass it off as one's own'. Few students would make a deliberate attempt to 'steal' another person's work in this way. However, unless you are very careful to make a clear distinction between your own ideas and words and those read in books, articles or from other sources, plagiarism can occur in your essays.

The most effective way to guard against plagiarism in your work is to ensure that you adequately *reference* any material that you have taken from another source, whether it be ideas, arguments or information. Even if you have related it in your own words (paraphrased it) you still need to indicate where you came across it, as in the following example:

> How we organise the layout and activities in an early years setting is not random, but indicative of the learning theory that underpins practice (May, 2011).

If you wish to introduce a *direct quotation*, that is the exact words, phrases or sentences from something that you have read, you must be more specific. For example:

> 'the reasons why our settings look as they do – why they have role-play areas, sand and water play, and an outside area for example – are not random. Each aspect of the early years setting is based on a theory' (May, 2011, p. 2).

The quotation is contained within inverted commas and the reference gives details of the actual page where it can be found in the original text. The source has been properly attributed and it is clear to the reader that these are not your words. The intellectual property of others may not only consist of words on a page but also extends to diagrams/tables of statistics/illustrations/recordings etc. Again, unless you provide the appropriate credits, use of such material could be viewed as plagiarism. Many institutions use plagiarism filters for students, such as Turnitin, which can be a great tool for improving academic writing as well as for helping you to avoid plagiarism.

It is important to remember that the work you submit must be substantially yours. Although you may derive very useful ideas, and even ways of expressing those ideas, from the people whose work you read, your own work will be judged on what you have done with this basic raw material. It should be evident that you have attempted to interpret, make sense of or reorganise the ideas that you have encountered, synthesising them into something uniquely yours. Not only will this impress your tutors, but it will also provide a unique opportunity for you to leave your mark upon the subject you are studying.

HANDY HINT

Avoiding plagiarism in your essay writing

The easiest way to avoid plagiarism in your work is to ensure that, when making notes, you clearly identify where your information comes from.

When making notes from books or other sources always include essential reference details, such as name of author, date of publication, etc.

It might help to use different coloured pens to distinguish between your words and ideas and those borrowed from someone else.

When paraphrasing material that you have read, try to translate it, as far as you can, into your own words and concepts. It is not enough just to change the occasional word or phrase. Your work should carry the clear imprint of your own mind!

Your institution may use plagiarism software detection, such as Turnitin, to help you with your essay writing.

Summary

This chapter has established the importance of giving time and careful consideration to correctly interpreting the wording of the essay title and planning an appropriate, structured answer. The following chapter builds upon this foundation by examining other forms of assignment, such as reports and case studies and the final 'polishing' process of editing, referencing and proof-reading your work.

Further reading

Check out your institution's study support services; also, try searching for guidance from other university websites, for example, at: www.essex.ac.uk/.../How_to_improve_your_academic_writing.pdf.

Books by the following authors all contain very useful advice and guidance on themes discussed in this chapter:

Stella Cottrell
Alice Savage and Patricia Mayer

MunLing Shields
Derek Soles and Nigel Warburton

Reference

May, P. (2011) *Child Development in Practice: responsive teaching from birth to five.* Abingdon: Routledge.

6 Further writing: reports and case studies

Introduction

In addition to essays and examination questions requiring essay-writing skills, students may be set other types of assignment. This chapter therefore considers tackling a more open assignment, as compared to an essay, and the writing of reports and case studies. Later in the chapter there is a section related to referencing text and setting out a bibliography based on the Harvard referencing style.

Mastery of essay writing will remain fundamental, as the rules and basic structure can be applied and adjusted to fit other forms of assignment. When tackling any assignment, it is important to follow the guidelines offered by your own institution – especially the assessment guidelines – as these will help you to plan and present your work in the way that is expected. Allow time to think, plan and practise, and use any feedback from your tutor to improve upon your skills constructively.

Planning the writing for an assignment brief

The essay question or title is often the starting point for an academic assignment. However, because Foundation Degrees and similar courses are designed for those working with children, often assignment briefs/instructions are given instead. These do not give a specific title but set seemingly wide parameters for the assessment task. Such assignments offer a more flexible framework than an essay title to suit the circumstances of students situated in different workplaces, but initially they can be daunting because they do not tell the student *exactly* what to do; decisions have to be made as to how to tackle the task. You may feel that working towards a specific essay title is easier, as fewer decisions have to be made, thereby limiting the number of likely mistakes. So, after reading the assignment brief, it may help to clarify the task if you create a working title from the details of the assignment. It may provide a focus and structure for your work and match your personal workplace experiences. For example, look at the wording of this assignment:

> Carry out a critical analysis of an interaction between one child or a small group of children and an adult, related to supporting a child's literacy learning. This could be recorded electronically or written as a detailed observation record. The assignment should identify strategies used to support language/literacy and be analysed with reference to the effectiveness of the strategies used. Evidence from a range of reading must be demonstrated in the assignment.

When you read this, it is clear that there are some things that you must do for this assignment, and it is always useful to list these, or at least highlight key words in the text:

1. critically analyse an interaction between a child(ren) and adult
2. identify any *effective* strategies to analyse that were used to support literacy
3. provide evidence of reading (through accurate referencing).

However, you will still have to make a number of decisions. For example:

- What method will you use to record the talk?
- Which child or group of children will be recorded?
- When should you record the talk – during a directed lesson time, or during free time?
- How much of the talk should be recorded?

Some choices are more academic and may be dependent upon the age range of the children involved; different strategies will be needed for different groups of children. This last point will direct your independent study – some students will need to find reading resources related to the early years, others related to primary- or secondary-age children, or perhaps to children with additional educational needs.

Other questions also arise from the term 'literacy learning'; thinking about the meaning of this will also create choices, although all are likely to revolve around speaking and listening initially, as this is implied by the 'recorded' nature of this assignment. However, this phrase could also be interpreted as leading children towards the development of reading or writing skills. By creating your own working title you can capture the relevant parts of the assignment while making it personal to you. Here are some examples of titles drawing upon the assignment brief:

- Example 1: An essay reflecting upon the key strategies used to promote quality literacy learning during story time in an early years setting.
- Example 2: A critical analysis of effective strategies used to support literacy learning during discussion time in a Year 1 classroom.

- Example 3: A critical analysis of strategies, including effective questioning techniques, used in a History lesson with a group of Year 6 pupils to enhance the literacy development of written work.

If you do create your own title, then go on to tackle this as an essay in the way described in Chapter 5. Start by making a plan, collect your content material, devise your structure and start writing! Remember, if you do this, that the title is not a set title, so you must ensure that you are still sticking to the details of the assignment. Keep the assignment instructions and marking criteria in front of you to make sure that you do not go off at a tangent and fail to meet the requirements! Essay titles and assignment briefs set the parameters of the material that you should cover and give vital information about what sort of approach you should take to that material. Ignore them at your peril!

HANDY HINT

When you start writing the assignment
Write out the assignment details in large print and underline key words.

Keep this within your vision as you plan, read and then write. This should help you to keep all your writing relevant to the topic.

To summarise, essay and assignment questions are structured in a way that:

- gives you guidelines about what is relevant and what isn't
- gives you clues about how to view the topic, whether to be descriptive, critical, make arguments for and against, comment on teaching/learning strategies, etc.
- asks you to think about particular terms or concepts
- aims to provoke a response in you, as the writer.

Writing reports

The previous chapter set out the basic ways to approach essay writing, particularly looking at the structure of academic work. Most assignments can be tackled in this way, unless, of course, the assignment starts with 'Write a report . . .'.

Report writing has a similar basic structure to essay writing, in that both have a beginning, middle and an end, although there are some important and significant differences. Report writing is by nature a form of writing that explains some aspect of work or an event that has been investigated, observed and critically analysed in a more scientific and formal manner.

The presentation of a report looks different from an essay, as it uses headings and sub-headings to guide the reader and can include relevant diagrams or charts and bullet points, both of which are not acceptable within an essay. Whereas an essay ends with the main points being drawn into a conclusion, a report ends with recommendations for future action based upon the conclusions drawn from the report findings. The style of a report is even more impersonal than that of an essay, with a need to convince the reader on the basis of facts and evidence rather than ideas and opinions.

Planning the report

It may help to think of yourself as a private detective or as a lawyer for the defence as you plan and write your report. You will need to track down and collect relevant information to use in your report and provide evidence to support the interpretation of your analyses of activities and events. This will help to provide sound arguments for any future changes or action that you may wish to make. Initially, reading the report question to determine what is required and then breaking down the report into manageable sections will help you to deal with each part of the task in turn. Consider this example:

> Produce a short report (3000 words) focusing on a specific area of communication in your workplace. This should take the form of an appraisal of what this involves and how communication could be improved.

Picking out the key words and determining what they mean to you might help you to make a start. 'Communication' is a broad term covering many aspects of human behaviour, but you are required to be 'specific'. It may be to your advantage to mind map communication in relation to your workplace and consider the different forms of communication that could be used for the focus of your report. For example, look at the diagram in Figure 6.1.

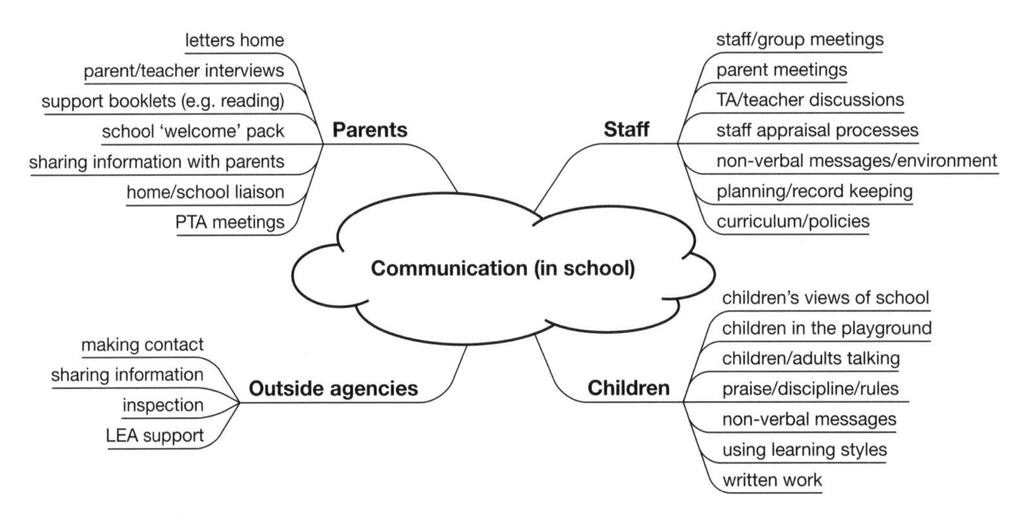

Figure 6.1 Example of a mind map of communication in the workplace

There are many choices that you could make at this stage; for example, you could investigate how staff communicate with each other in school, or how the adults communicate with children. You could narrow this further by examining one aspect, for example, by looking at record-keeping procedures. The next step might be to think again and create another mind map, or, if you prefer a linear approach, to write a series of questions that need to be answered; each in turn may lead to further ideas or questions (Figure 6.2).

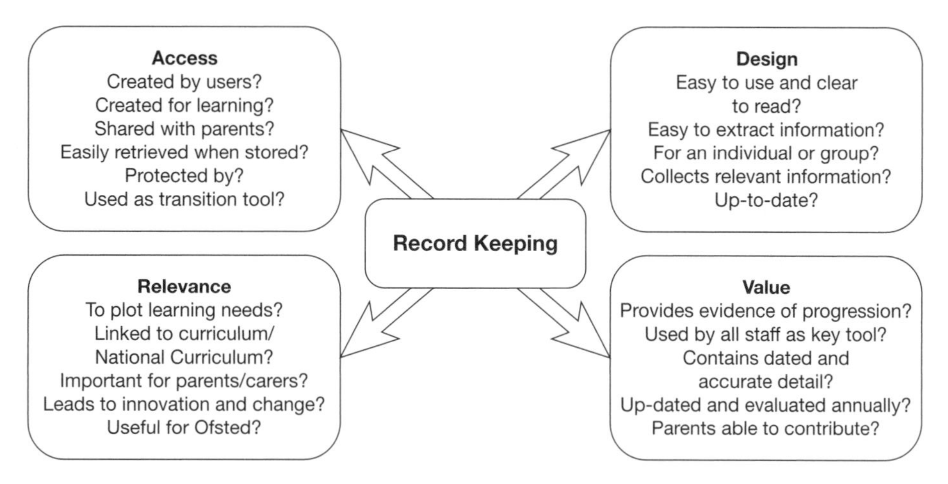

Figure 6.2 A linear approach to assignment planning

Asking and answering questions forms the basis of this type of investigation. Although you may not be able to answer within your report all of the questions contained in your mind map, it is the attempt to get at the core of what is happening that drives research and leads to a clearer understanding of why some things work and others don't. These questions should not be presented within your work, but used to start the reflective process in your thinking.

HANDY HINT

Becoming more reflective and analytical

Questions posed might result in answers that begin like these:

1 Letters home are an effective way to communicate with parents/carers *because* . . . This is significant to the child learning *because* . . .
2 The significance of good relationships between staff and effective communication is . . . This is supported by evidence from . . . *because* . . .
3 The workplace record keeping documents are . . . This provides evidence of . . ., which indicates . . . *because* . . . and . . .

Note that the word 'because' can be a trigger for reflection. Looking for the reasons why something works or doesn't work and backing this up with evidence from (a) reading, (b) the workplace, (c) your thinking will help to make your writing more 'academic' and 'analytical'.

Now, looking back to the wording of the report assignment, two further key ideas were included, namely that (1) an 'appraisal' should be carried out, and (2) there should be 'suggestions for improvement'. Many students at the beginning of study do not wish to appear to over-criticise their workplaces or colleagues. They believe that making recommendations for improvement might be perceived as being critical. However, this should not be the case. Looking with new eyes and trying to find small ways to improve even good practice is a positive step, not a negative one.

Having considered the report assignment question carefully, you can now focus on collecting the right evidence and reading relevant documents that will show your knowledge, understanding and ability to critically analyse events and the purposes behind the way adults in school help children to learn to communicate. Plan and study in the same way that you would for an essay assignment. Although you will be writing about real experiences and practices, you will need to link these to other writers and theories to show that you understand the ideas and purposes behind these practices. Simply writing about your experiences will not be enough – reflection and analysis are vital elements in academic writing, as, of course, is reference to reading material.

HANDY HINT

Avoiding description in your report and essay writing

It is tempting to write reports by just describing what you observe, or by describing the work of key writers in the field. However, analysis MUST go beyond the mere description of your activities and observations.

So, as you write, STOP and ask yourself questions, such as:

1 What does this really mean for the people involved?
2 Why does this work/not work in practice?
3 Are there any alternatives to this way of working/seeing things?
4 Which reading also describes what I see?
5 How could practice be improved in the future?

By answering such questions within your writing, your style is likely to become more analytical.

Structuring the report

As previously suggested, essays are usually written as one continuous prose document, whereas reports are broken down into sections by the use of headings and sub-headings, and may also include bullet-pointed lists. Reports are also written in a more 'scientific' way, with short sentences and clearly set out evidence. Your own institution may provide specific rules on how reports are to be set out. The chart on page 86 shows the structure of a report.

Numbering the report

Most institutions will be satisfied with your report being organised with headings and sub-headings. However, you may be required to use a numbering system. If this is the case, you need to number only the main section, as shown on page 87. You will need to identify three levels of numbering: the major headings or sections, the sub-headings or sub-sections and further supporting sub-sub-headings. Each major heading or section is given a single number (1, 2, 3, etc.); the sub-heading numbers have one decimals place (1.1, 1.2, 1.3, etc.) and the sub-sub-headings have two decimals (1.1.1, 1.1.2, etc.). It is not as complicated as it looks! Ideally, the numbering should be inserted after you have written the report and as you proof-read your draft.

Case studies

Field studies, participant observer reports and qualitative descriptive research are examples of phrases used to describe case study reports. All may be approached in a similar way and all will test your problem-solving skills. The structure of a case study is very similar to that of a report, the main differences being the content and the style of writing. A report usually focuses on resources or curriculum ideas, as in the communication report example given above, whereas case studies usually centre upon individuals or groups of people. A case study takes a more holistic, humanistic approach and the style, although formal, is rather more personal than that of a report. Although a case study can be of any length, sometimes a case study style will be required for a dissertation or longer essay, and the structure of the case study can be a great help in planning a lengthy piece of writing.

Writing a case study offers a way of using work-based experiences to gain understanding and knowledge for future use in a real-world situation in a chosen field. Mature students have the advantage of being able to utilise previous experience to write case studies based on familiar environments with familiar people. They are therefore able to draw upon a collection of relevant evidence.

Case study evidence

In focusing upon an individual or a group, a range of evidence can be collected, offering opportunities to explore a situation or series of events as it relates to people. Here, you will be faced with two problems: what evidence is important and how should you interpret the evidence?

As a researcher, a student trying to answer 'how' and 'why' and to find the 'truth', you should consider the way in which you will influence the outcomes of your study as a result of your own beliefs and attitudes. Whatever evidence you collect will be open to analysis and interpretation and could therefore be biased. This fact will be one of the limitations of your study, and you should acknowledge this very

Structuring a report

Section	Content and headings
Preliminary section	**Title page** ■ Title of the report ■ Your name ■ Your college course ■ Date **Table of contents** (if required) ***Short* summary of the report**, with general background details
Main section *(If you are required to number your report, you number ONLY this section; keep numbering as simple as possible.)*	**Introduction: this *may* include** ■ A statement of the 'problem', or the aims of your report. ■ What you plan to do in order to provide some answers (the data-collection methods, e.g. observations, interviews, etc.). ■ The purpose of the report – what you hope to achieve. ■ Who the report is written for and how it might help them. ■ The limits of your report – what you will not be able to do.
	Findings, with discussion ■ Use headings and sub-headings for each part of your report. ■ One paragraph usually contains one main idea. ■ Relevant diagrams, tables, graphs may be included to make the evidence clear. ■ Analyse your findings and relate them to your reading. Point out the most significant findings within your evidence – what does it all mean? ■ Analyse your findings in relation to what you expected to find and whether this agrees with the views found in your reading.
	Conclusions ■ Do not be tempted to include new material or ideas. ■ State the most important points again, and why these are significant. ■ Check that the conclusions match the aims of your report. **Recommendations** ■ Suggestions for future action that may improve the way people work/learn etc. ■ Write these suggestions in order of priority.
Supplementary section	**Bibliography** ■ Make sure that this is set out in the required style. **Appendices** ■ Any information that you have gathered that contains too much detail to be included in the main body of your work, but is nevertheless relevant to your report. ■ Label and number each appendix.

A report's 'Contents' page, showing the numbering system

Section	**Headings and numbering**
Preliminary section	**A Report on Communication in a Year 5 Classroom** Title page Table of contents Summary of the report
Main section (*Number only this section, as indicated*)	1.0 Introduction 1.1 Aims and purpose of the report 1.1.1 Report audience 1.2 The methods of data collection 1.2.1 Observations 1.2.2 Interviews 1.2.3 School policies 1.3 The expectations and limits of the report 2.0 Key findings 2.1 Communication in the classroom 2.1.1 Current practices 2.2 Spoken communication 2.2.1 Children talking 2.2.2 Adults and children talking 2.3 Written communication 2.3.1 Encouraging children's writing 2.3.2 Adults' use of written communication 2.4 Other forms of communication 2.4.1 Non-verbal messages 2.4.2 Communicating beyond the classroom 3.0 Conclusions 3.1 Significant findings 3.2 Limitations of the report 4.0 Recommendations 4.1 Creating opportunities to communicate 4.2 Developing the policy for speaking and listening 4.3 Celebrating achievement
Supplementary section	Bibliography Appendices Appendix 1 Appendix 2

briefly in your writing. The amount and type of evidence that you collect for a case study could be so wide and varied that any choice you make will affect your final results, so try to go for a balance of evidence that seems to be fair and offers an all-round view. The list of possible evidence includes:

- observations
- interviews with children and/or adults
- test results/progress reports
- examples of children's work
- workplace documents, polices, records
- photographs, taped oral recordings, videos
- lesson or group support plans, evaluations, notes.

You should consider the ethical issues implied by all of these. Always check the procedures related to the collection of evidence and obtain relevant permission. Most importantly, of course, you should always maintain the confidentiality of any child or adult by collecting evidence in such a way that the individual cannot be identified.

HANDY HINT

Including photographs in your case study
Photographs may be used as evidence in case studies. To maintain confidentiality, get permission before you take photographs, and take photographs in such a way that any individual's face cannot be identified. Back or side views of the individual usually make identification more difficult. This looks better than covering up any faces after the photo has been produced.

Getting started on the case study

In deciding on both the collection of evidence and the interpretation, you will be directing your own learning, formulating questions, solving problems and taking responsibility for your own study. This is therefore a great opportunity to find out more about something that you either are already interested in or know little about! The starting place should be thinking about what you want to find out. Mind map or list the questions that you need to answer, as in the example in Figure 6.3.

Stop here and consider one aspect of your workplace that could be the focus of a case study. Quickly note down the relevant aspects that you could use to help you put a case study together in a mind map or in linear form, as in the example given in Figure 6.3: include the topic focus, the child/group, the evidence to be collected and the questions that you would wish to answer. Now decide whether anything requires action or improvement and consider where you might find relevant

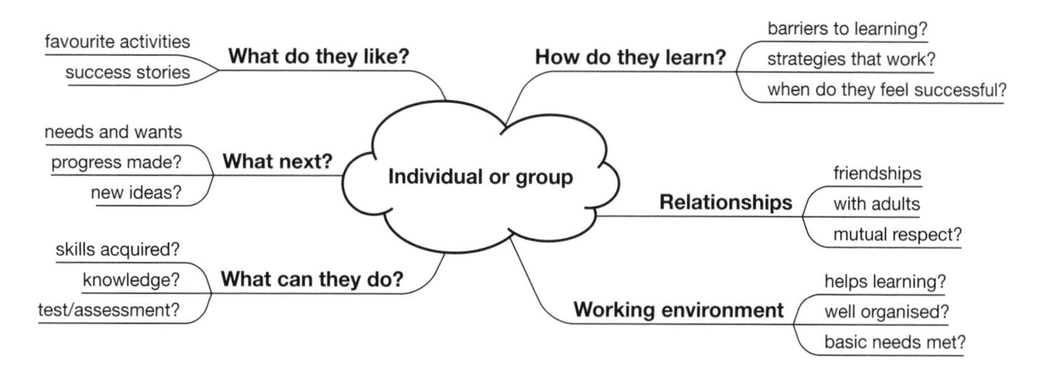

Figure 6.3 Example mind map of questions to research for a case study

reading resources. Completing such an exercise will help you to become more analytical and reflective!

As you plan, and start to analyse events, you might begin to find some answers to the questions that you pose. Relate these to theory in the same way as when writing essays or assignments. As you work, your case study may raise further questions – this is an important part of study, and you should include implications for further research at the end of the case study.

Structure of the case study

Case study structure (see page 90) is similar to report structure, but when writing you can include your personal reflections and show your own point of view clearly. These make the case study more personal and give a 'human interest' aspect and style.

The finished product

When your writing is finished you will doubtless feel an enormous sense of relief – but try to resist the temptation to hand it in there and then. Most work will benefit from editing. View the essay, report or case study that you have just completed as a first draft and don't be afraid to read through it. If possible, it is a good idea to leave a time gap between finishing and reading, as this allows you to look at your own work in a calmer, more neutral and more critical way. At this stage you need to be honest with yourself and ask some questions of your work.

Questions about language

- Is my meaning clearly expressed?
- Do my paragraphs have a central topic?
- Do they work effectively?

Structuring a case study

Preliminary section	**Title page** ■ Title of the report ■ Your name ■ Your college course ■ Date **Table of contents** (if required)
Main section	**Introduction: setting the context** ■ Give the aims of the study. ■ Outline of the main points to be covered. ■ List the resources, materials used. ■ Give information on the individual/group (ages, type of learner, etc., but maintain confidentiality). ■ Provide a description of the environment (classroom or centre).
	Findings of your case study, which may include: ■ How you collected evidence – observations etc. ■ Why you collected evidence that way. Benefits and drawbacks. ■ Examination of the approaches/strategies used so far (short history of the individual/group). ■ Which resources/approaches were used, and their effectiveness. ■ The responses of the individuals/group/others. ■ Benefits to the individuals/groups/institution. ■ How your study links theory to practice. ■ Obstacles and problems you faced.
	Conclusions ■ Brief summary of the case study. ■ Recommendations for future practice. ■ Limitation of your study. ■ Suggestions for further study or development.
Supple-mentary section	**Bibliography** ■ Make sure that this is set out in the required style. **Appendices** ■ Any information that you have gathered that contains too much detail to be included in the main body of your work, but is nevertheless relevant to your case study. ■ Label and number each appendix.

- Do they follow on?
- Have I stuck to the expected number of words?

Questions about content

- Are my central points clear?
- Have I presented a coherent position?
- Is my argument convincing?
- Have I given enough supporting material/evidence to make my case?
- Do I like what I have written and have I included some of my own ideas?

You may well find that you need to make some alterations, for example:

- cut things out
- give further detail or expand on points
- re-phrase sentences and restructure the order and length of the writing
- clarify or define terms that are not clear in their meaning or application.

Editing may seem painful at the time, but it is almost certain to be worthwhile and it is something that you should consider building into your timetable. The planning sheet on page 92 may help you with your task, or you could adapt or use the information contained in the tables to design your own *aide memoire* for planning work, whether this is for an essay, a report or a case study.

Assignments, reports and case studies: last word

Reading about writing is not the same as being actively engaged in the work. Hopefully, you will now have some idea about how to approach these tasks, but there is no better way of learning than actually doing it yourself. Plan carefully and seek advice from tutors and support staff – take a plan or draft with you so that your tutor can give advice and support you in moving forward. When you receive your marked work, do not be disheartened by any adverse comments – use them as a way of learning and moving forward. In this way you will learn from your mistakes.

Reading reports and case studies will help your writing style and it is worth noting that many journal articles are written as reports or case studies. When you go online, searching for journal resources for your next assignment, stop and consider the structure of the writing: is it an essay, or a report or a case study? Through reading, your writing will improve as you absorb the academic style, but you are more likely to improve if you make yourself aware of different writing styles as you read.

Planning grid for writing

Title:

Hand-in date: **Tutor:**

PLANNING CHECKLIST

Planning	**Thinking**	**Writing**	**Final plan check**
Check assignment	Found focus of work	Made plan for writing	Check assessment!
Time set aside to work	Sorted main points	Selected references	Check marking criteria!
Mind map/plan started	Know main arguments	Paragraph ideas clear	Stop reading!
Search for resources plan	Thinking critically	Overall structure clear	Go over writing
Plan library visit	Reflecting on evidence	Start writing	Continue writing!

PRELIMINARY WORK

Key words to consider from assignment details	
Key texts and authors *with page numbers* (*save bibliographic details*)	
Other resources to review	
Evidence collected	
Main conclusions and future action indicated	

FINISHING AND POLISHING CHECKLIST

Meets the set criteria?	Clear arguments shown?	Makes sense?	Bibliography correct?
Expresses my ideas? correct?	Connections shown?	Checked spelling?	References
Interprets information?	Word limit correct?	Checked presentation?	**READY TO HAND IN?**

Bibliographies and referencing systems

When writing an essay or any other form of academic report it is important to indicate where your information has come from. There are several reasons why this is so:

- it shows your tutor what you have read
- it enables others to check your references
- it ensures that you acknowledge the work of others
- it avoids accusations of plagiarism (see Chapter 5)
- the practice provides a network of information for those studying in a given area.

This last point is important. The practice of providing references and lists of sources and published material that you have used enables those interested in the area to build up a picture of relevant material. In other words, it is a practice designed to share information, promote research and protect ideas. It is as important for students to follow this good practice as it is for established academics.

There are several ways of acknowledging the source of material in your essays. You will, no doubt, notice the different methods used when you are reading. Some authors use numbered footnotes at the bottom of each page, some prefer to list all their sources at the end; in both of these instances there will need to be a separate bibliography (a list of publications that has been referred to in the text). HE institutions adopt a single system to provide a uniform, standard way of referencing; you should check what this is in your own institution. One of the most commonly used systems is the US Harvard system. However, books are now only one of several sources of information available to students that require referencing and a bibliography, as many students use sources that are available online as well as those available from the library. This may explain how variations in referencing rules have come about as each new information source has been made to fit an older system. The bibliographic rules for other sources are based upon the Harvard-style rules for books, but they can be more difficult to work out initially; details may be unavailable or you may seem to have more information than you need. However, the basic rules for referencing and setting out the bibliography remain the same, so it is worth spending some time to becoming familiar with the basics.

The basics of Harvard-style referencing

When you cite a book or publication in the main body of your text, put the author's surname and the date of publication in brackets in the appropriate sentence or at the end of it, like this:

Jones (2013 p. 6), or if at the end of a sentence like this (Jones, 2013 p. 6).

When including a book in the bibliography at the end of an essay, you need to add information to enable the reader to find your source. The entry should be set out in this order:

- last name of the author(s) or editor and initials (*if the name is that of an editor, include* (ed.) *after the initials*)
- year of publication (*put this in brackets*)
- title of book (*this should be in italics*)
- edition (*if not the first edition*)
- place of publication
- publisher.

The idea is that the reader will be able to quickly see which book you are referring to by looking at the author's name and the year in which the book was published. The best way to explain this is to give some examples. Suppose you want to use a book by Simon Robertson, entitled *Children and Adults Learning Together* published in 2013. This is how you could do it:

> It is suggested by Robertson (2013) that children and adults studying together will provide additional ways to learn using an apprenticeship approach.

If you have quoted directly from Simon Robertson you must make this clear. Use *inverted commas* and give a page reference:

> Robertson suggests, 'good use can be made of the apprenticeship approach by encouraging adults and children to learn together' (Robertson, 2013, p. 90).

In your bibliography you must give the full details of the book so that others can find it if they want to, making the title separate from the other details by using italics:

> Robertson, S. M. (2013) *Children and Adults Learning Together.* London: The Imagine Press.

Sometimes you will come across ideas, quotations etc that one author has already taken from another. In this instance you should reference the book where the information was found, not from where it originated.

For example, you have read about Robert Brooklyn in a book by Hassan, so within your own work you might write:

> Brooklyn argues children and adults should study together (cited in Hassan, 2013, p. 61).

And usually in the bibliography you would list Hassan as your reference, and also give the full reference for Brooklyn (check this requirement with your tutor).

Setting out the bibliography

The bibliography will usually be the last page of your assignment, although in some work it might be appropriate to include a bibliography at the end of some sections. The books should be listed alphabetically according to the authors'/editors' last names. When using more than one book by the same author, start with the book published first. The following is a short sample bibliography:

Bradford, H. (2012) *Appropriate environments for children under three.* London: Routledge.

Gleason, J. B. & Ratner, N. B. (2013) *The development of language.* London: Pearson.

Lee, C. (2010) *The complete guide to behaviour for teaching assistants.* Thousands Oaks, CA: Sage Publications.

Spooner, W. (2011) *The SEN handbook for trainee teachers, NQTs and teaching assistants.* London: Routledge.

The following are some points about the bibliography:

- Note the colon between place of publication and publisher and the comma after the surname.
- You should be able to locate the necessary information on the cover/copyright page of the book that you are referencing.
- If you are typing, use italics to indicate the title. If writing by hand, then underline the book title.

If creating a bibliography is new to you, then trying making a point of looking at the referencing strategies and the way the bibliography is set out in the books that you are reading. This will help you to learn this procedure.

Referencing online sources of information

Many students go online for research, as the internet is available 24/7 and many resources are available for study purposes. However, even more important than the referencing rules for an online source is the reliability and accuracy of its content. Carry out basic checks to determine that what you are using as a reference in an academic piece of work is relevant and based on real evidence. Anyone can publish on the internet, and some sites are dubious!

Basic questions to ask are:

- What am I looking for? *Prepare a list of key words before you log in!*
- Does this come from a reliable source? *E.g. a university (.ac or .edu) or organisation (.org).*
- Do the writers have any authority? *Where do they work? Who pays them to write this? Is the writing biased in any way?*
- Is this information dated? *Some items have been lingering in cyberspace for years!*
- Is this information relevant? *What country does it come from? Does it represent the views of a few people, or of many?*

Once you have found a good source of information, as with reading books, note down all the details for future reference before you log off, or save the link to your favourites/bookmarks. The internet changes frequently, and things quickly 'disappear' as they are updated, so make sure that you collect all the necessary information on the day you view the web.

When referencing online data, follow the Harvard style by giving the author's name and the date, where known, or, if no author is given, the title of the web page and the date, and if there is no title, then give the owner of the site. If no date can be found on the website, indicate this in your referencing. Here are two examples that illustrate some of these points:

1 'the evidence from Webwise (2013) indicates that . . .'

2 'information suggested by Teaching Assistant (no date) . . .'

The corresponding bibliographic entries would read:

1 Webwise (2013), BBC, [online]. Available at: http://www.bbc.co.uk/webwise/0/ (Accessed 15 March 2013).

2 Teaching Assistant (no date). Available at: http://www.teaching-assistants.co.uk/ (Accessed 14 April 2013).

Note that you should include the exact URL (website address) and the date when you visited it. If you can do so, avoid splitting the web address across two lines of text. If this is not possible, split it after a forward slash. Here is a summary of the information that you need for the bibliography:

Author/editor:	Or page title if no author or organisation name is given.
Year of publication:	'No date' if date of publication is not given in source.
Title:	Use italics.
[online]:	Indicates types of medium; use for all internet sources.
Place of publication:	If available.
Publisher:	If ascertainable; or give the name of the organisation responsible for maintaining the internet site.
Accessed date:	Date on which you viewed or downloaded the document.
Available at:	Give the full URL (the WWW address).

Referencing from web pages can be problematic – provide as much information as you can, remembering that the main purpose is for the reader to be able to find your source material. To ensure that the web address is correct, consider copying and pasting it directly from your internet browser, rather than typing the details. Give more than just the web address in the bibliographic entry – follow the Harvard system as closely as possible.

E-journals and e-books

Journal articles or whole books are available online, and if you reference from these, for bibliographic purposes follow guidance for referencing books, rather than for web pages. Add the 'Available at' statement at the end, like this:

> Parsons, E.C. and Carlone, H.B (2012) 'Culture and science education in the 21st century: Extending and making the cultural box more inclusive.' *Journal of Research in Science Teaching.* Vol. 50, Issue 1, pages 1–11. January 2013 [Online]. Available at: http://onlinelibrary.wiley.com/doi/10.1002/tea.21068/full (Accessed 10 January 2013).

Often, students make reference to government department papers that are available online, and the rules for including these in either referencing or the bibliography are the same, for example:

> DfE (2012) *National Occupational Standards for Supporting Teaching and Learning: Teaching assistant.* Available at: http://www.education.gov.uk/schools/careers/traininganddevelopment/staff/standards/b00203854/nos-for-stl/units-for-particular-jobs/ta (Accessed: 10 December 2012).

Multimedia

You may wish to reference recordings of films or educational programmes, or off-air recordings of news or programmes that have been shown on television. It is relatively easy to track down information for television and radio broadcasts if you have the title or series title. Similar rules apply, and examples are given below.

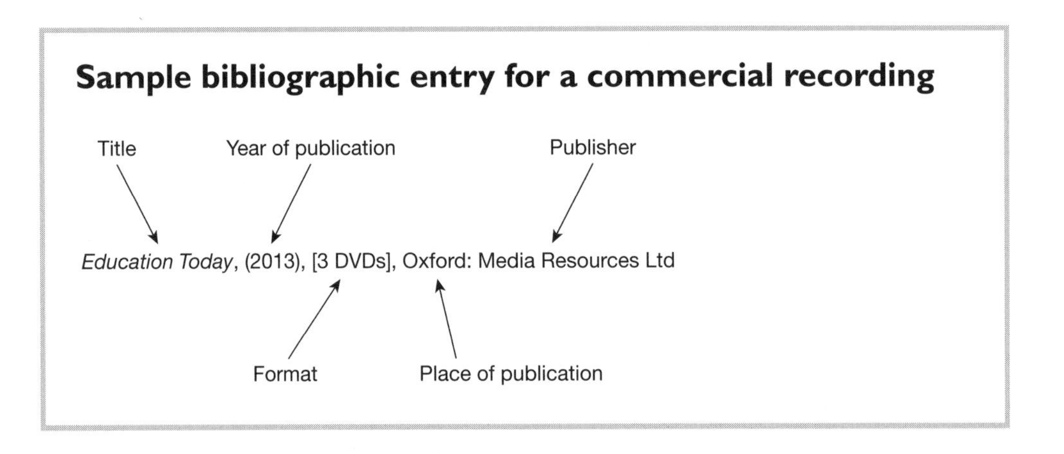

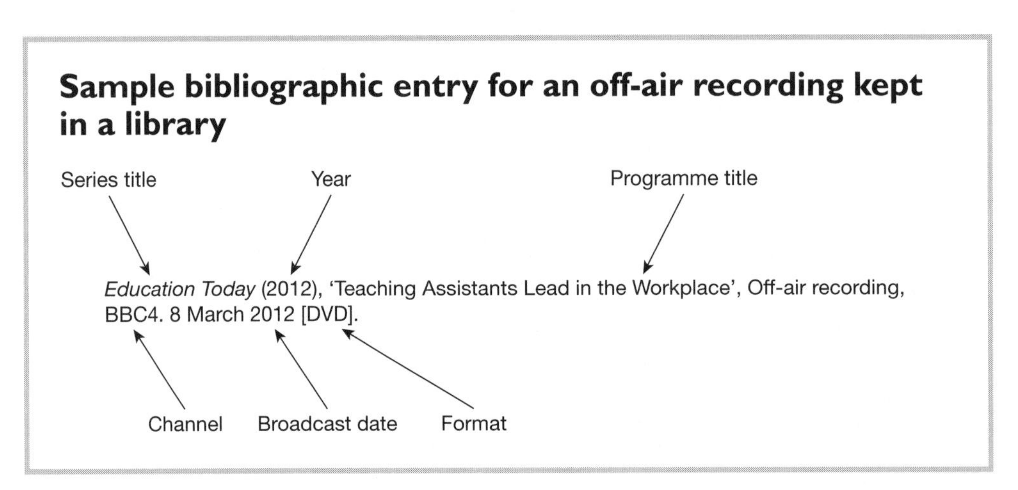

Sample bibliographic entry for multimedia – government YouTube interview

Munro, E. (2012) *Professor Eileen Munro talks about child protection.* 9 May 2012. DfE. Available at: https://www.education.gov.uk/inthenews/multimedia/a00198339/munro-review-of-child-protection (Accessed: 23 July 2012).

Newspapers and unpublished material

The reference should be cited in accordance with the Harvard system, e.g.:

Helpster (2013) argues that too much GCSE course work is unnecessary.

Bibliographic entries should conform to the format author/year of publication/title of article/title of newspaper/date of issue/page number, as in the example in Figure 6.21.

Unpublished material may include reports and information gathered from lectures or PowerPoint presentations (although you should check that your tutor approves of using such material). The referencing procedures are the same as for other resources already described, but in these instances you will need to replace the publishing details with the statement 'unpublished'.

Sample bibliographic entry for an online newspaper article

Helpster, W. (2013), 'Students under fire', *Educational News*. 23 May [online]. Available at: http://www.ednews.co.uk/2205220 (Accessed: 26 May 2013).

Summary

This chapter has expanded upon some of the conventions that should be considered when writing specific assignments, reports and case studies. Although they are similar, each has its own style and purpose and gives opportunities to develop different skills. This chapter has also established the basic rules of referencing and of creating a bibliography, both of which are essential elements in presenting a professional piece of work. You will need to practise these aspects of academic work and regularly review the bibliographic layout for the different information sources that you use. The important message here, which is worth repeating, is to keep full and accurate records of everything that you read!

Further reading

For more about avoiding plagiarism, see Chapter 5; for more about developing search strategies, see Chapters 2 and 8 (for Boolean logic).

For an exhaustive list of Harvard referencing rules read:

Pears, R. & Shields, G. (2010) *Cite them right: the essential referencing guide.* Basingstoke: Palgrave Macmillan.

There are many online resources and study guides that will provide you with further advice about reports and case studies. The Plain English Campaign (www.plainenglish.co.uk/free-guides.html) has guides available on its website – check out the section on writing reports.

7 Portfolios and other assignments

Introduction

Although essay writing remains one of the most popular forms of HE assessment, the value of using different assessment processes to provide a variety of experiences and allow students to develop in different ways is also very strong. In this chapter, some of these alternatives will be explored and the main characteristics described. These include:

- Portfolios (including graduate skills and action planning)
- Work-based assignments and tasks
- Oral presentations
- Displays and poster presentations
- Dissertations and longer assignments
- Timed essay papers.

Portfolios

A portfolio is the general name given to a folder that contains an organised collection of materials and evidence, often linked to workplace investigations or personal development. Although they are generally produced as hard copies, some universities are encouraging students to keep e-portfolios, but the basic process and purpose remain the same. The portfolio collection is designed to demonstrate how a student has developed a range of skills over time and may contain elements of self-assessment. The content of the portfolio might be restricted to a curriculum subject, to a child or group of children or to a specific area of professional development. It might be conceived as a case study (see Chapter 6), or be more informal. A portfolio requires an introduction and section notes, but might also include:

- the results of questionnaires with analysis
- observations and photographs

- action plans and notes
- completed tasks that have been set for the course of study
- discussion documents
- workplace documents
- readings and reflections
- timed entries, as in a journal or diary
- work completed by others, e.g. children in school
- a bibliography.

The quality of your writing, in terms of reflection and analysis, is an important aspect of all academic work; however, one of the main features of a portfolio is the organisation of the material. Planning the layout of your portfolio in the initial stages takes time, but may pay off later – and be less worrying than leaving the organisation to the last minute. Use file dividers to sort out your work as you go along. If the portfolio is to be completed over an extended period of time, dating work, observations and events may be important to establish chronology. The ethics of your work, where it impinges on others, will mean that confidentiality must be maintained, so think carefully about how you are going to present your findings and indicate clearly that ethics have been considered. Lastly, if you are producing work on a computer, then save all the pages, even after printing, just in case you need to make last-minute adjustments. Figure 7.1 shows the steps required to create a portfolio of work.

Portfolios for personal development

Increasingly, students are required to submit evidence at the end of their programme of study to demonstrate development in graduate skill areas, and this is likely to be in portfolio form. This type of collected evidence is commonly called a Personal Development Portfolio or Plan (PDP). As graduate skills have become more important to universities, students are expected to be more aware of their developing skills during study and to keep a record of their progress. Unlike essay or assignment writing, which have comparatively short production times, maintaining a collection of evidence requires regular short bursts of time, similar to keeping a diary. Whether the portfolio is a personal record of progress or a longitudinal study, you should consider its purpose carefully and collect relevant samples to show progress and development over time.

Graduate skills

As stated in Chapter 1, a skill is something that you have learnt to do, and can do, usually without thinking about it too much. Graduate skills are considered by tutors

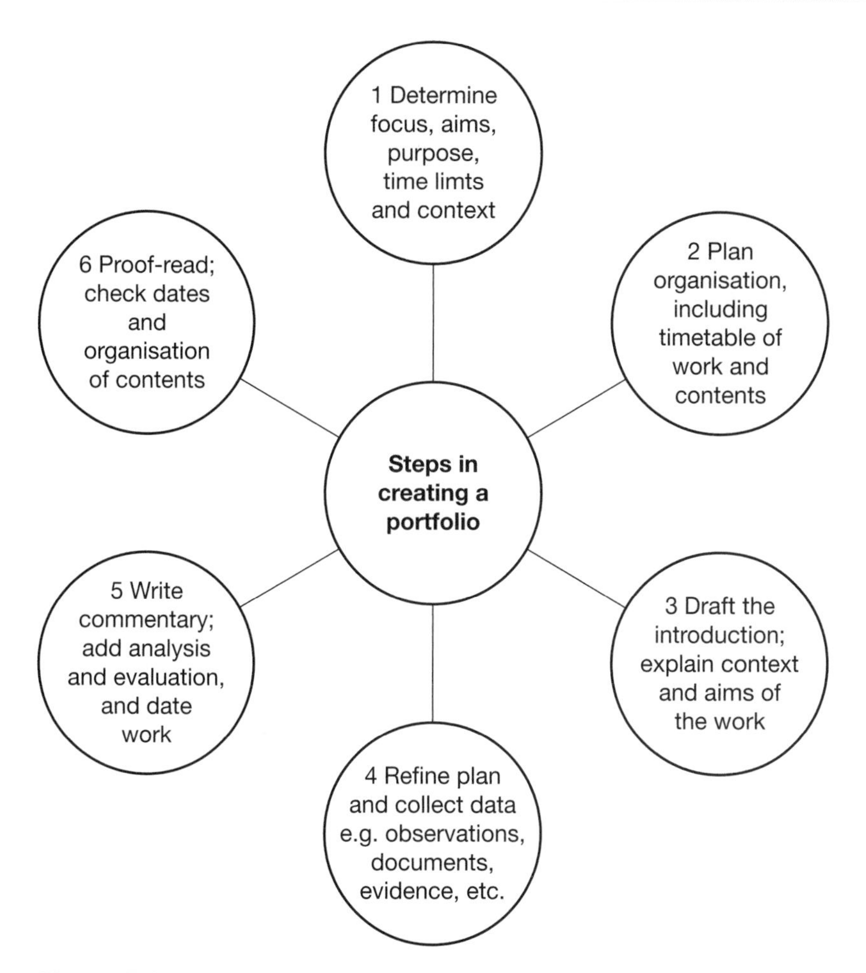

Figure 7.1 Steps in creating a portfolio

important academic and professional skills required for effective study in HE and are also often identified as the skills needed to be successful in the workplace. As such, employers as well as educational institutions may be interested in your progress.

Graduate skills fall into the categories of:

- communication
- working with others
- improving your own learning and performance
- academic skills.

Universities and colleges may identify different aspects of these graduate skills as important, but the core skills remain essentially the same. Educational institutions also vary in how they expect students to maintain the portfolio record of their progress. Electronic portfolios enable students to record progress online, thus eliminating the need to maintain a written portfolio. Software programs for this purpose usually have a built-in structure with pre-set questions and guidance for completion. Other institutions expect students to create and maintain their own record in written form. One way to structure this activity is shown below.

Portfolios: maintaining a record of personal development

Steps	What to do
1 Preparing *Set up the portfolio*	■ Buy large ring binder with file dividers. ■ Create title page with your name, date, etc. ■ Check exactly what your portfolio should contain and create a contents guide. ■ Start to date everything!
2 Planning *Create the action plan*	■ Identify the skill area(s) you wish to develop. ■ Create an action plan, using SMART targets (Specific, Measurable, Achievable, Realistic, Timebound). ■ Identify the strategies that you are going to use.
3 Monitoring *Keep notes on how your plan is working*	■ Regularly collect evidence of your progress. ■ If what you are doing goes well, note this down. ■ If you hit problems, note this too, and suggest ways that these problems can be overcome.
4 Evaluating *Complete your notes by writing a statement of your progress*	■ Note what worked and what didn't. ■ Note the support given to you from fellow students and colleagues or resources that you find. ■ Note what you are now able to do that you couldn't before and how this benefits yourself and others. ■ Indicate what you think you should do next to continue the development.

Regardless of the way in which you record your progress during study, demonstrating your development will be the most important factor. This will require initial planning, recording of experiences and monitoring and evaluation of progress over time.

Action plans

The planning stage is always an important stage in completing any piece of work successfully. Action plans are usually the approved method for this type of exercise in a PDP. They are just what the name suggests – a plan for action. To increase your chances of success in completing any set of plans, ensure that they contain SMART targets, as this helps them to stay focused and relevant. SMART targets are designed to be:

S	**Specific**	*Exactly* what do you hope to do?
M	**Measurable**	How will you know if you are successful?
A	**Achievable**	Are you really able to do this?
R	**Realistic**	Can you do this in the time/with the resources that you have?
T	**Timebound**	Set time limits on what you do.

SMART targets should be the centrepiece of any planned action, and you can identify them within your essay plan, within your workplace plans or even in everyday personal plans such as going shopping! If you pause for a moment and think about the daily tasks that you undertake and apply SMART 'logic' you will find that it exists naturally to get any task completed efficiently and effectively. So, using SMART action plans deliberately will assist in the completion of any task that requires planning.

Action plans are usually constructed in a grid form (see the examples below). They can be simple or more complex, to suit you and your circumstances.

Decide how you want your action plan to look, and then create an action plan template to use over time. Getting this right at the beginning should save time later. As you complete the 'actions' directed by each action plan, create another action plan, so that over time your portfolio grows, providing a unique collection of evidence detailing your personal development. Obviously, you cannot record every aspect of your progress and will need to determine priorities, matching the requirements of the programme for recorded evidence with your personal development needs. All students have different strengths and weaknesses and will have to plan to meet their individual needs, so make your choice of development a personal one. Consider the skills that you feel require some effort to grow, and plan development carefully by deciding exactly what you need to do within your time-frame.

To help you to get to this stage, create a mind map first so that you can narrow your focus and be more specific about what you wish to develop. There is guidance available on the internet – many universities have set up websites for their students with advice on developing graduate skills. You can easily access a range of these using a search engine such as Google and select those that seem most appropriate for you. To get you started, however, the following is a list of some of the 'communication skills' that you will need to develop further during study:

- writing: essays, reports and other academic forms of writing
- speaking: being clear and expressive, taking part in discussion, giving short talks

Action plan

Specific targets	Specific area for this action plan:	Date:
	My main aim will be to develop:	
Measurable	My present strengths in this area: what I can do already:	
	My weakness is this area: what I would like to improve:	
	How I will know that I am making progress:	
Achievable	Why I need to do this:	
Realistic	What I will have to do:	
	Resources I will need:	
	Support I can expect to receive:	
Timebound	How I will prioritise and set time limits:	Completed by?
	1	
	2	
	3	
Progress notes	Comments:	Date:

Final evaluation of action plan results:

Date:

- listening: gathering meaning (during lectures) and being a thoughtful, reflective listener
- giving and receiving feedback: being sensitive to others, but also able to be assertive in stating your views
- using body language: being able to 'read' others and being aware of the signals that you give out.
- using images: using diagrams, pictures, statistics and multimedia
- using e-communication: email, texting, blogs and wikis, etc.

You may feel that you are already confident in several of these skills and competent in using them, but others might not feel so secure, especially within an academic context. Skills will develop naturally with experience and practice, and action planning creates the opportunity for you to determine when and where such experience and practice will take place. Doing something once, for example, giving a talk to a group of students, may not be enough for you to become proficient; therefore, monitoring and thinking about the 'next step' become important. SMART targets should aim to create small, achievable steps that over time will get you to where you want to be. Don't try to run before you can walk!

Action plans
(Keep them SMART!)

Start date	Specific target	Resources and tasks to complete	Indications of success	Finish date

HANDY HINT

Saving time with action plans

If you are not completing your PDP online, then you can save time once you have designed your action plan by printing off or photocopying several copies ready for use.

You can then fill in the details by hand, so remember to leave space for handwriting.

This will allow you to add dated comments and demonstrate how you monitor progress over time.

Portfolio evidence

Action plans are not always sufficient on their own to provide the evidence of development required and you may need other documents and work-based evidence to prove that your action plans are not just made-up pieces of paper. It is tempting to collect everything at first and fill up the portfolio quickly, but you should be selective in your evidence, remembering that the aim is to show progress. Without being too repetitive, collect evidence regularly and annotate and date it. The following are some suggestions for evidence to collect:

- tutors' mark comments indicating aspects for/of improvement
- examples of your work, including photographs, plans, use of IT
- examples of work from those you support, e.g. children's work
- appraisal notes or other reports on your progress
- your own reflections and evaluation of tasks.

Depending upon the subject and purpose of the portfolio, some sections may require evidence of your reading, with appropriate reflection and analysis. This may be something that you plan to complete on a regular basis, so build this into your way of working.

Structure of the portfolio

Putting together a portfolio requires initial organisation. Although some students collect work and then organise it, planning ahead will save time. Graduate skill-based portfolios can be organised under the graduate skill headings, with each section then being ordered chronologically. However, you may find that some skills are developed together – for example, communication is often linked with team working. In order to help the future reader of your work this problem needs to be solved early on. Writing an introduction and explaining how your portfolio is organised is one way to do this. Your file dividers could then be organised chronologically, to show periods of development, rather than subject development. To create a balanced portfolio, include a general evaluation of the whole as a final section. The structure might then be as shown opposite.

Whether a portfolio is being constructed for a PDP or another purpose, the structure and process will be similar. Tutors will be interested in how you develop strategies and monitor progress and in how you evaluate both the strategies and the progress made. These three important steps – develop, monitor and evaluate – should be clear throughout your work.

A portfolio is a difficult document to page number, as it is constantly being added to and changed. To overcome this problem, the whole needs to be organised into sections and listed clearly in the table of contents so that items can be easily

Structure of a portfolio as a collection of evidence	
Opening section	Title page ■ Name, course title, date ■ Contents page (it is not necessary to have page numbers, but still make this your last task!)
	Introduction ■ Aims and rationale of the portfolio – the 'why?' ■ Brief description of the subject content of your portfolio ■ How you intend to collect evidence
Main section *Divided into parts with each part containing:*	Action plans/indication of section content ■ Followed by relevant evidence ■ Monitoring of progress ■ Evaluation of progress made ■ Next steps for development (if relevant)
Concluding section	Evaluation ■ What you have achieved over time, your personal view ■ Brief summary of successes and failures ■ Your plans for the future
Supplementary section	Bibliography ■ Any texts that you may have used to illustrate your work

located by the reader. This task can be completed towards the end of your course and prior to submitting the portfolio. Do allow time for this, as it always takes longer than you think it will!

Work-based learning

Foundation Degrees are work-based studies, so you may be required to carry out work-based tasks in addition to other assessment tasks. These tasks might form part of a portfolio collection. The tasks are set to give you an opportunity to demonstrate your skills in the workplace and to share them with fellow students and colleagues. In addition, any work-based task will help you to focus on the understanding and knowledge required to become proficient in your job and will assist you in analysing the theory behind what you do on a daily basis, and may be used as evidence in assignments. Tutor input and discussion with other students during university or college sessions might provide ideas for tackling tasks, but you will probably be expected to complete your own research – reading around the subject, collecting evidence – during your own private study time.

Although work-based tasks may not be assessed using the same criteria as essays or other assignments and may not have a set word limit or clear framework, they are often a vital part of the course work. It is important, therefore, to get know the expectations and requirements of your institution, as each work-based task may be recorded differently, with some records filling just one side of A4 paper and others requiring greater length. Do not worry if your work-based task records seem to vary in length or style. This activity is often very individual, both for the person and for the workplace. Find out what is required and what is acceptable, and work accordingly.

HANDY HINT

Recording work-based tasks

The most important aspects of the task should be noted. For example, reflect upon:

- What you have learnt from the task itself.
- What you have learnt about others by completing the task.
- The insights you have gained about your workplace.
- What the contributory factors to your task result were.
- How the task findings may affect your future actions.
- Links to the readings you have used in your studies.

If you regularly plan, prepare and record what you do, you should not have to engage in a sudden flurry of activity towards the end of the course in order to catch up on any missed opportunities to write or to carry out tasks.

HANDY HINT

Planning work-based tasks

- Draw up a timetable and work plan – set deadlines.
- Identify specific tasks that need to be carried out.
- Negotiate time at work to complete the tasks.
- Read around the subject.
- Gather resources or materials needed.
- Carry out task, collect evidence as required.
- Write up tasks; structure work, proof-read and evaluate task.

Giving oral presentations

Giving a presentation involves more than just standing up to talk, although this in itself is usually the biggest hurdle to overcome, especially if you are not used to speaking to a group of adults. However, giving a presentation is just like writing essays or preparing assignments – once you know how, then you can become more confident in your performance.

Preparation and planning

You need to consider two things at the start of your planning – the audience you will be addressing, and the content of your talk.

The audience matters in a presentation, as you will need to pitch your talk at their level. Whether talking to familiar faces or to strangers, you will have to determine your choice of vocabulary and content. It is also important that any non-verbal messages that you send are thought out before the presentation; for example, consider your clothes. Do they give the impression that you are serious in your work or that you can't really be bothered? Such things may not seem important to the final outcome, but they are worth considering because they can also affect your behaviour. How you stand and face the audience will also send messages – making eye contact and smiling suggests that you are confident and in control, even if you feel like running away! Think about these things before the day of the presentation, and practise.

The content of the presentation may be predetermined by your coursework. Read the presentation brief carefully, just as you would an essay question. Decide what is too important to be missed out, using the assessment criteria as your measure. Next, it is important to get the sequence right so that you can reach out to your audience and get them to follow and engage with your argument. Plan for the presentation in the same way you would when working on an essay or other assignment – mind map, find appropriate and relevant reading and carry out some investigations of your own. By ensuring that you have a good grasp of the material, you can be confident of being well prepared to answer any questions at the end of your talk.

HANDY HINT

Giving oral presentations

The simple rule for remembering the structure of presentations is:

1 This is what I am going to talk about.
2 Now I'm talking about it.
3 This is a summary of what I talked about.

Rehearse your presentation to include visualising how you are going to walk up to the front, smile, give your talk, answer questions and walk confidently back to your seat.

That way, you programme yourself to go through the whole sequence of events successfully.

Structuring the presentation

You should aim for a polished, professional presentation, and the structure should give you this. Many students fail to introduce their talk clearly and are unsure of how to finish. Ensure that the beginning and end of your talk are clear and crisp, and that the middle is interesting and well researched. Don't just read your work, as this can come over to the audience as dull and uninteresting. Summarise your main points on file cards and use these as prompts. Keep the cards in the correct order by punching a hole in one corner and tying them together with string or cord (in case you drop them!). If you prepare a PowerPoint presentation, you can print out the slides with your notes and use these as your prompt. The printout will also give you a clear reminder of what will appear on the next slide. Whiteboards and flip charts can be prepared in advance too, and will contain the main markers to help structure your talk.

Whatever the visual presentation you choose to use, or even if you do not use any visual aids, as you begin to talk look for 'friendly faces' on both sides of the room, smile and imagine that you are just talking to them. This may help you to feel more confident and should at least help you to look confident. The main points to remember when structuring your presentation are shown below.

Structuring a presentation	
Introduction	■ Smile and introduce yourself, thanking audience for attending. ■ Tell the audience the title and the aim of your talk. ■ Tell the audience how long you will speak for. ■ Tell the audience that you will answer questions at the end. ■ Let them know if there are handouts available before/after your talk (if appropriate).
Main section	Sequence carefully, building up your argument. You may want to include some of the following points: ■ outline of the present situation/research regarding your topic (include your relevant reading!) ■ the current problems/issues ■ details of any options that have been tried out in research or by you ■ details of any strengths and weaknesses of current practices.

Conclusion	Include a short summary of the main points you have made, also: ■ suggest proposals/recommendations for future action ■ suggest how this might be implemented ■ suggest further reading or research. Close your talk with thanks and then ask for questions. After responding to the questions, thank the audience again, gather your materials and return to your seat.

Supporting your presentation

Tutors will expect to have details of your talk either beforehand or at the time of the presentation. These are probably best organised in a folder containing a written version of your talk, copies of your notes, PowerPoint slides (if used) and any supporting resources in an appendix. Make sure that the written version contains the references to reading and research that you used for your talk.

PowerPoint slides and other visual aids

Most oral presentations set as an assignment are of short duration, usually ten to fifteen minutes with an additional five minutes for questions. It is important that you keep any PowerPoint slides or visual aids to a minimum, so as to keep within the time limit. Keep these simple and clear enough for the whole room to see. Slides with headings enable you to talk and fill in the details. Quotations, pictures, cartoons, maps and charts are also valuable visual aids, as they tend to hold the audience's interest for longer than just text. Be aware of possible distractions. For example, if the projector makes a noise, remember to switch it off when you are not using it. Whatever equipment you decide to use to support your talk, plan some practice time and test it before the presentation. It can be very unnerving to stand up and find that the equipment won't work for you!

The following are additional ideas to support your presentation.

- Collect words on a flip chart (prepare this before or complete during your talk).
- Show a selection of children's work.
- Use an interactive whiteboard.
- Demonstrate a well-tested (by you!) experiment.
- Use the audience (you may need to ask for and cue some 'volunteers' before the talk!).

Displays and poster presentations

The primary aims of these two presentation methods are brevity and clarity. You will need to get to the core of your study and present the information in a readable and visually attractive format. This demands skills that will test your understanding of the main issues of a subject, as well as your design skills. Plan for these types of presentation in the same way as for any other academic assessment – firstly by carefully reading the display or poster brief and checking the size and scope of your work, and secondly by creating a plan so that you work effectively on the task; and then follow up with reading and research in your workplace. This will help you to identify your goal early on and begin to focus on the important elements needed for your work.

There are some basic points to consider when creating either a display or poster presentation:

- Include your name, poster/display title and study purpose somewhere on your work (this may be required on a separate sheet).
- Make the main text readable from about 1–1.5 metres distance.
- Include text and visual images so as to draw in the audience.
- Make sure that any image captions are clear and not too small.
- Use chunks of text and/or bullet-pointed lists rather than longer passages of text.
- Include quotations, if appropriate.
- Unless you are 'artistic', stick to basic primary colours and basic design.
- Keep it simple – use clear, basic fonts that are easy to read.
- Consider a mind-map design, or numbered panels to sequence the content.
- Mount the work with attention to detail, so as to give a professional finish.
- Don't forget to proof-read your work – a misspelt word on a poster is very eye catching!

The hardest part of creating any poster presentation or display is in deciding what to leave out. Don't clutter your work with too much detail – but concentrate on showing your understanding of the main points of your argument/subject and on making this clear to the audience.

Supporting your work: the rationale

Students will probably find that an accompanying rationale is required to support the display or poster, and this gives the opportunity to show thinking processes and study in more detail. This should be structured in a logical way, with:

- clearly stated aims and objectives
- a main section containing evidence of reading, analysis and logical arguments to support the content of the poster/display
- a conclusion and summary of main points.

The two parts of your work – the display and the rationale – will be used to assess your knowledge and ability in the area assessed. It is therefore important that they complement each other and that an equal amount of energy and effort is put into both parts of the task.

Displays for the workplace

If you are working towards a Foundation Degree in an educational area, you may find that your display is school-based and either aimed for children to read and/or produced by children. The completed display can then be photographed and presented for assessment. The basic rules of the display will be the same as those listed previously, although the content and text will be directed to the curriculum area and the age of the children you are working with. The most successful displays have an interactive element and engage the children in thinking or in practical activities. To include these elements, you might consider posing questions in your display or having a 3D aspect to your work. If this is the case, remember to have any hands-on activities at a height that the children can reach, and pay attention to any health and safety issues that might arise. If your display is successful in engaging the interest of children you can also expect it to receive some fair wear and tear, so use tough or replaceable materials where necessary, and photograph it before the children get to it!

To make the display interactive, here are some basic ideas that you could develop:

- Create flip-up 'windows' with answers to questions or key words underneath.
- Have tear-off quiz sheets for the children to respond to the display.
- Create a tactile area so that the children can 'feel' as well as see.
- Let the children put key words in the right places (e.g. use labels) using Velcro strips or Blu-Tack.
- Include books, objects or experiments in the display, placing them on a table in front of it.
- Have moveable parts to your display – for example use dials or sliders.

If you work in an educational setting, then it is likely that you have experience of creating displays to help you with your design and planning. Enlist the help of colleagues and consider negotiating for space and materials.

Other practical types of assessment might also have a work-based theme, such as making a learning resource, and these should be approached in the same manner. Ensure that you know what is required, keep it simple but effective and be prepared to justify the choices you make with supporting evidence from reading as well as from your personal experiences.

Dissertations and longer assignments

Typically, essays and assignments have a set word count of 2000–4000 words. Dissertations vary in length, generally being between 6,000 and 12,000 words, and are based upon a small-scale research project or enquiry carried out by the student in the workplace. At some stage in your academic study you will be required to produce such a longer piece of work.

Writing a longer piece of work is a great opportunity to demonstrate all the skills you have acquired over time and to really get to grips with a subject that interests you. In carrying out research or writing up a short independent enquiry you will need to identify a question or problem and then choose ways to try to find answers at first hand, rather than just from reading. There are many ways of beginning this process, and colleges will support students; but if you are in any doubt start by mind mapping and listing all the questions that surround your topic area and then create a statement or title that sums up what you want to know or test. It is easy to imagine that research is something grand and important, but it is often the small questions that are really interesting and inspiring. Keep your research SMART – make sure that it is manageable, realistic and within your own time limits. Use the chosen theme of your writing to guide your decisions regarding initial reading and research.

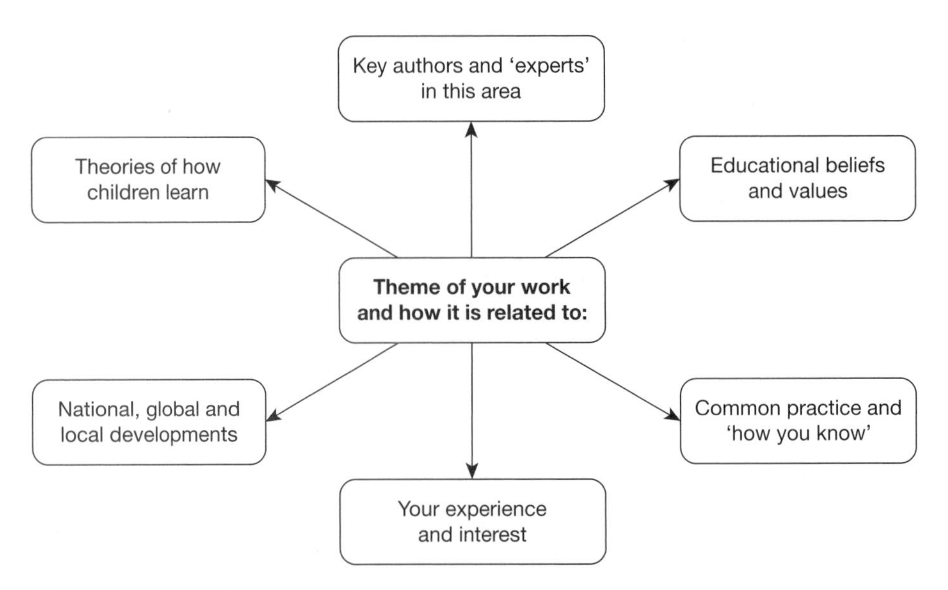

Figure 7.2 Spider diagram for a dissertation

The length of a dissertation can seem daunting at first, but good planning will make the whole thing manageable! It is important that you set yourself goals for completing the different parts of your work as you go along, so that you don't panic when you get close to the hand-in date. Set targets for each part of the work you need to undertake, such as reading, research and thinking, and consider setting up a timetable to keep you on task. Build in rewards, and stick to your plans!

A longer piece of work is usually structured in such a way that you can view each part almost as a separate 'assignment' when it comes to writing up your work. Consider the typical breakdown of an independent enquiry shown below.

A guide for structuring an independent enquiry (8000 words)

	Title and contents pages Abstract	
1250 words	Introduction	Set the scene for the reader, with context and main aims of your enquiry.
2250 words	Literature review	Critical review of what others have written about this topic.
1250 words	Methodology	How you planned your research, considering the strengths and weaknesses of the methods used.
2250 words	Findings	Analysis of what you have found out.
1000 words	Conclusions	Bring the main points together, and also look to the future.
	Bibliography and appendices	

Each part can be tackled separately and the different parts do not need to be completed in the same order as they appear in the final structured form. Some work can be drafted earlier and kept ready for the final polish at the end. The grid in the timetable on page 118 offers guidance on the possible order of tackling the various tasks. You may find that you are working on several parts of the work simultaneously, so save each section separately on your hard-drive (plus back-up copies!) so that you can access the part that you want quickly and easily when you need to work on it.

Timetable for writing a dissertation/independent enquiry					
Section to be tackled	**Reading completed by**	**First draft completed by**	**Proof-read and ready to print by**	**Notes**	**Done?**
Literature review					
Methodology					
Findings					
Introduction					
Abstract					
Bibliography (keep records as you work)					
Contents page etc.					

Contents of a dissertation

The following is a brief description of the contents of a dissertation – although it is advisable to check the specific requirements with your tutor. Often, the whole process starts with a proposal form, a copy of which is given to the tutor so that the progress of the work can be monitored over time. A proposal form might ask questions like those shown opposite.

Sample proposal form for a dissertation	
Name	Date
Possible working title:	
What is the main area of focus? How is this relevant to your workplace?	
What are the main enquiry questions? Why?	
Relevant literature to be researched; prominent authors/research/journals/other	
Methods of collecting data/making enquiries. How? Valid and reliable?	
Support/resources required (including people)	
What might you expect to find out during your enquiry?	

Writing the abstract

This is simply a summary of the work that allows the reader to get a good idea of the content before reading the whole. Libraries and online journals use abstracts to help readers find relevant texts without having to read the full article (see Chapter 2), so check some out to see how they are written and consider the writing style of several abstracts to help you in composing your own.

Introduction

As in essay writing, the introduction sets the context for your writing by describing your workplace and the people involved in your research and giving the aims and objectives of your study. It also gives a brief overview of the current status of the topic, i.e. it sets the scene for the reader. Remember to keep details general and consider the ethics of your research, not least by maintaining the confidentiality of all those involved.

Literature review

This provides you with the opportunity to show just how much you know about your chosen subject through reading and your own analysis of the material. Use books, journals, government documents, workplace policies, research documents, records and any other relevant texts to illustrate your reading and to support your own thinking. In particular, you should be looking for patterns and themes in published literature. Is there general agreement or are there contradictions in the books you have read? Has anyone else tried to answer the same questions that you want answered? Does the literature reflect what is actually happening in your workplace? This should all feel like familiar territory, as this is the usual stuff of essays and assignments! At some point, you will need to stop reading and start writing. Keep an accurate record of all your reading, even the works that you have rejected, so that time is not wasted looking for 'lost' quotations or re-reading rejected articles. The literature review provides the foundation for the enquiry and the starting place from which to ask new questions.

Methodology

In this section, explain what research methods were chosen, and why. Research methodology describes the ways in which first-hand information is gathered. Some methods rely on the researcher gathering a fairly large number of simple responses to analyse in table or graph form and other methods rely more on the interpretation of more individual responses. These two types of information are referred to as quantitative and qualitative data, and are collected using such research tools as:

- questionnaires and surveys
- interviews
- observations
- historical documentation and evidence
- logs, diaries of events and recorded responses to events
- case studies
- action research.

Each of these methods has its own set of 'rules' and approved way of working, so find out more about the method that you choose. Whatever method you select, the issues of reliability and validity need to be considered. Reliability is concerned with the truth and accuracy of the research. There is always a dilemma, as interpretation of events, conversations or documents is always open to bias and different people will record different things. Validity deals with the question of 'so what?' How relevant will your findings be to the workplace and to others? To help solve some of these problems, you should use at least two different methods of information gathering. This is known as triangulation, a term applied to any enquiry that uses two or more methods in its research. You should initially explore the advantages and disadvantages of your chosen methods before deciding which to use for your research. Include a brief statement indicating the ethics of your work and how you have maintained confidentiality when collecting data.

Findings

In this section you can analyse your findings, giving the reader the information that you have collected, and show how you have interpreted it. Here, analysis is more important than description, so spend time on demonstrating your ability to cross-reference information to the literature review and support your views with the material that you have collected. Illustrate your writing with charts, diagrams, statistics and quotations drawn from your research, but keep the bulk of the 'raw' data in the appendices.

Conclusions

Summarise the main points, linking them to the main aims stated in the introduction, and show how each of them offers insight for future action or future research. Explain in a tentative but confident way what this means for you and for your workplace.

Lastly, remember to proof-read your work – or better still, get someone else to do this task – and to check the details such as the title page and the bibliography. These details are important and will affect the final mark. Often dissertations need to be submitted as a bound piece of work, rather than in a loose-leaf ring binder. University and college libraries or bookshops usually provide binding facilities. Remember to allow time to do this before the hand-in date!

As stated above, although longer assignments can seem daunting at first, they can also be exciting – they provide an opportunity to write about your own passions and interests. The tutorial support offered to students when writing dissertations means that you can be fairly confident that your work will meet the criteria for the course.

HANDY HINT

Saving your work

Remember to back up all your work (consider emailing work to yourself as an additional way of saving it safely). There will be little sympathy if your computer crashes and your work is not available at the last minute!

Also, do not forget to build in time to print your work, as this can take longer than you think it will!

Seen exam papers

Many institutions set seen examination papers for some courses, although sometimes these are called 'timed essays'. Students are given a copy of the question paper before the day of the examination so that they can prepare for the test – commonly, there is a gap of two or three weeks between receiving the paper and sitting the exam. The process of revising is therefore more straightforward than for 'unseen' papers, as students know the questions and can revise and practise writing the answers, but in many ways the preparation process is the same. Having the paper beforehand just takes some of the fear away! You may ask why tutors bother with an exam at all, if everyone knows what the questions are going to be. One explanation is that examinations provide one of the few occasions when tutors can be certain that the work presented is a student's own. In some strange way, too, some students do not feel that they are truly 'academic' unless they have been tested through an examination. Therefore, if you are set a seen paper as part of your assessment procedures, follow all the advice given for planning essays and consider how this may fit into the preparation steps detailed below.

Steps to answering a seen exam paper

Preparation prior to seen paper date

1. Plan draft answers carefully (mind map or create a linear plan).
2. Check that each response will match the question set.
3. List key points, relevant authors, work-based evidence, recent research.
4. Plan to give a structured response to the question – get your information in order (introduction, middle section, conclusion).
5. If possible, work with other students by discussing and checking each other's work and sharing ideas. Do not, however, share any draft answers electronically!

Working towards the set date

1. Reduce your structured plan to the minimum.
2. If using a support sheet that you can take into the exam room, record the names and publication dates of key authors to use in your answers.
3. Note any details of your own experience that you wish to use in your answer.
4. Practise writing the answer from your plan. Work out how much time you will be able to give to each question – how much can you physically write in the given time?
5. Check again that your answer matches the question.
6. Check the marking grid: will your response to the question match the marking grid criteria?

Immediately prior to the set date

1. Check that you have working pens and pencils, plus any other permitted items.
2. Remind yourself that you have prepared well, so there are no surprises in store.

	3 Use any relaxation exercises/thoughts that keep you focused and in control.
When you arrive	1 Arrive in plenty of time and wait outside the room until asked go inside. 2 Make yourself comfortable, then concentrate on listening to the tutor's instructions. 3 Check the exam questions again before you start writing and focus your response on answering the question. 4 Check your timings, do not over-write on one answer and leave little time for your next question! Pace yourself carefully. 5 Read through each question at the end of your set time, correcting punctuation and spellings as well as factual errors as you go.
Afterwards	You may have a feeling of anticlimax and then start to remember all the important things that you left out! It is too late, so do not waste time worrying at this stage. Trust that your preparation carried you through and that you have done enough to achieve the grade you want.

Summary

Variety in assessment procedures offers an interesting range of academic tasks that should enable you to approach professional development using a range of skills. Whereas you, as an individual, may prefer one form of assessment over another, by using a range of assessments the programme of study offers opportunities for everyone to shine in one or more different areas. The approach to assessment should be consistent, however, with thought first being given to the assessment question and then being followed by careful planning and finally with proof-reading. All assessment procedures should have a clear beginning, middle and end, and if you keep this in mind as you work, then the chances of success are increased.

Further reading

As for the previous chapters, plenty of advice is available online for the various assignment types, and other publications may augment the guidance given here. Check out Chapter 5 for general writing tips, and refer to Chapter 8 for strategies for tackling examination papers and for searching for resources online.

A search for the work of the following authors may provide further inspiration:

Daniel Girard (oral presentations)
Martin Cox (oral presentations)
Mark O'Hara et al. (dissertations in education)
Dr Bryan Greetham (dissertations)
Robert K. Yin (case studies)
Gary Thomas (case studies and dissertations)
Michael Bassey (case studies).

8 Challenges: examinations and searching for resources

Introduction

This chapter will help you to find ways to meet the challenges involved in tackling examination papers and in searching for relevant and appropriate resources for assignment tasks.

No one really enjoys sitting exams, apart perhaps from those people who have found ways to be good at them! Certainly, for most students the thought of being tested, judged and perhaps falling short of the mark evokes feelings of trepidation and anxiety. However, despite those feelings, which are experienced by teachers as well as students when 'put on the spot', there are tried and trusted techniques that you can learn that will minimise your anxieties and maximise your chances of success in examinations. Considering the nature and purpose of exams, and methods of organising your time and study materials, will help to make revision a more effective and less arduous experience.

In the second section of this chapter some tried and trusted ways of searching for information are explained. Searching for relevant and appropriate reading and other resources can sometimes take up a considerable amount of time. Sometimes a student can be left with a feeling of being overwhelmed by the number of resources found, or feel that nothing of any use has turned up in the search. Developing academic search skills may save you time and help you to find the resources that you need.

Why exams?

Why are exams difficult?

Perhaps the first thing to appreciate is that examinations and the revision that goes with them are 'challenging' because they require a student to be able to coordinate a number of quite different, though related, activities. These include many of the 'graduate skills', including time-management strategies, working well with others, making clear notes, finding relevant reading resources, as well as being able to think critically when selecting information and first-hand work-based experiences. Then, of course, there is the need to remember some critical facts! But take heart. With some instruction in the basic techniques and some determined, regular practice it is quite possible to become proficient in making all the right moves necessary to pass examinations.

How important are exams?

Perhaps the first place to start when considering examinations and revision is to find out exactly how your course is being assessed. In order to view your exams from the right perspective you need to have a clear understanding of how much of your course is marked on the basis of coursework and what proportion of marks are dependent on examinations.

The prospectus or the course handbook should contain this information. However, in some instances the procedures for assessment can be quite complex and you may find it helpful to approach your course tutor or director of studies to explain the details of the process of assessment for your particular course. It is particularly important to do this early on if you have a recognised disability, as then any necessary support procedures can be put in place. Once you understand to what extent your overall course result depends upon coursework and what percentage upon exams, you can start thinking about how much time and effort you should allocate to each so as to maximise your chances of doing well.

Preparing for the exam

One of the most common questions students ask about examination revision is 'When should I start revising for my exams?' They are often quite surprised to find that the answer is 'From the start of your study!' Ideally, the whole process of learning should, from the outset, be *active* and involve students in *reflecting* on and *reviewing* everything as they are being taught.

If you adopt this incremental approach, each new lecture you listen to, seminar you participate in or assignment you write is an opportunity to *appraise and revise* your current understanding (or lack of it) of your subject. Such a learning strategy, if you can maintain it, of course, makes the whole process of exam revision much easier, as it reduces the need to have to cram lots of largely undigested, unrelated information from your notebooks into your memory over a short period. By constantly 'upgrading' your understanding in this way you should achieve a working knowledge of your subject which will simply need augmenting to enable you to answer the questions on the exam paper.

HANDY HINT

Organising your materials for revision purposes

You can find more about making and organising notes in Chapter 3. Whether your notes are taken from lectures, textbooks, the internet or from personal observation, they will need to be *labelled* and *filed* in a manner that will enable them to be easily identified and retrieved. Here are some suggestions:

- Keep your notes for different parts of your course in separate ring binders or in sections separated by clearly marked file dividers.
- Always date your notes.
- Ensure that you record references as you make notes.
- Give each set of notes a brief, clear heading identifying which part of your course it relates to, the name of the lecturer or reference details of its source.
- Try to gather together lecture notes, handouts, essays, books and miscellaneous related materials for each of your subjects in a 'pack'. This should make it easier for you to access information for the purposes of exam revision.
- Reduce your final notes to a manageable size for revision, perhaps a mind map or spider diagram.

Organisation and study strategies

In practical terms, you will need to work out a method of organising your lecture notes and other study materials so that they can be related clearly to the subjects you are likely to be questioned on in the examinations. But how do you know what topics are likely to emerge in the exams?

Predicting the future by looking at the past and present

Actually, there are a number of clues or pointers that you can follow that will indicate to you what topics, if not the actual questions themselves, are likely to emerge in any given exam. Students who tend to do well in exams are those who have learned this art of predicting what is likely to occur on the exam paper, based upon the available evidence.

What topics were you supposed to have covered over the course of the year/duration of your course? You can usually find this out from a copy of the syllabus/course handbook. Compare this with the lectures and seminars that have been delivered over that period, as well as any assignments that have been set. By comparing these you should be able to gain an impression as to whether some aspects of your course have been given special prominence or if certain topics have been approached in a particular way. You can expect this emphasis to be reflected in the examinations, unless you are specifically told otherwise.

Studying past examination papers is an indispensable preparation for success in exams. Usually such papers, either as e-copies or as hard copies, can be obtained via the library or the Learning Resources Centre. Alternatively, you may find that your teaching department has a cache of past papers available in its section of the college/university website, sometimes with useful advice on how to prepare for the exams it sets. Looking closely at the questions that have been asked in exam papers in previous years will help you to identify which topics and issues crop up year after year. Very often the same *core* questions are being asked and are simply being worded differently, or require a slightly different emphasis. Having identified these core topics, and the main issues that have been highlighted in questions asked about them year on year, you can then decide which areas you need to study and which topics you can, perhaps, eliminate altogether from your revision.

If your course has a 'seen approach' to examination papers, where students get to see the exam paper prior to writing the answers, then past papers may not be made available. However, similar critical thinking is required in answering the seen exam questions, so read on, and also refer back to Chapter 7.

Effective revision strategies

Selective versus exhaustive revision

Some students panic at the thought of pegging their exam success on the kind of intelligent guesswork that is based upon past papers and course content. However, if you have sufficiently analysed the questions asked on exam papers over the last few years and understand where the questioners are coming from, this strategy can prove far more successful than attempting to learn everything you have studied over the past year or even longer.

A 'scattergun' approach – whereby students attempt to learn a little of everything they have studied on a subject, in the hope it will *somehow* help them to answer a set question – is not usually sufficiently focused to be of much use in an exam situation. An exam essay involves the same sorts of decisions that you make when writing coursework essays:

- What, essentially, is the question asking me to do?
- What are the most important aspects of this subject?
- What are the main issues it raises and where do I stand on these?
- What are my main arguments?
- What information, evidence and opinion will help to back up my position?
- What is the best way to structure this information in order to give an appropriate, reasoned answer to the question that has been set?

You can see that, in order to be able to provide such a clearly reasoned, well-structured answer to an exam question you have to be very *selective* regarding the sorts of material you choose to revise. You need to work out what information you need and how to structure it in order to answer exam questions *well before* you enter the exam room. Such preparation depends upon making fairly accurate predictions about the *sorts of topics* that are likely to be focused on in the exams and the *kinds of questions* that will be asked about these topics.

Obviously, such predictions are not infallible and you should prepare for the unexpected by revising some additional material in case the questions you had expected do not come up in the form you had anticipated. So, for example, if you have *three* questions to answer on an exam paper, you should prepare revision materials for at least *five* questions. This should give you a reasonable certainty of being able to answer the required number of questions, should some of the questions on the paper be awkward, unexpected or hard to understand.

Studying past papers is also useful, in that you become accustomed to the look of the exam paper itself. Information such as the instructions regarding how many questions to answer from each section of the paper can easily be misinterpreted under the stress of the exam. You can familiarise yourself with the language and phraseology used in exam questions so that you are less likely to be fazed when you see the same sort of terminology and phrases used in the actual examination. Taking the shock factor out of exam papers in this way is particularly important if these are your first-year exams or you are studying the subjects for the first time. It also gives you an opportunity to work with others, discussing past papers and course content and listening to and discussing ideas and then forming your own judgement as to how you can best prepare for the examination.

Taking stock of your study resources

Having identified what topics and questions are likely to come up in the exam paper itself, now consider how to best gather and organise the relevant material so that it can be understood, memorised and harnessed to answer exam questions. Topics encountered in exams are those that students have already studied; they may also have submitted written assignments on those subjects. So, a good starting point will be to gather together all the materials you already amassed on a subject – such as essays, lecture notes, notes from books and articles and any other sources of information – into a revision pack. Here is one suggested approach:

- Try to identify which of your notes contain the *essential* aspects of the topic you are revising and which contain less useful material. Give *priority* to some facts and concentrate on those, and weed out others that do not directly help you to answer questions in the exam.
- Aim to reduce this material to *core* facts under key headings, main points and essential reference material, such as name, date and title of work.

- Further condense these notes into 'memory cards' containing the main features of the topic you are summarising. Make these as brief and memorable as possible by using bullet points, numbering, colour, images and word play (such as 'Norwegians Eat Shredded Wheat' for the points of the compass) so that the structure and detail of that topic sticks in your mind.
- Look at these outline notes frequently, enlarge them and pin them up where you can't avoid seeing them, or record them in audio form. Look at and listen to these, testing regularly to see how much of the material you understand and remember. The more often you do this, the more this distilled knowledge will 'stick' in your memory.

Organising and analysing the results of revision

Next, *analyse* those materials to determine whether they contain the facts, arguments and references necessary for you to be able to answer the essential, core questions asked about those topics in the past papers you have studied. It is important, at this point, that you try to appreciate the subject in the round. You need to ask:

- What have my tutors identified as being most significant or relevant to my discipline when considering this topic?
- Are there any important ethical/moral/theoretical/practical/professional issues surrounding this topic? Do they have contemporary significance?
- Who are the main 'experts' who have written upon this subject? Have some been specifically referred to by my tutors, or have my tutors written on the subject themselves? Do the 'experts' have different opinions regarding aspects of this topic, and which do I agree with and why?
- What workplace experiences/observations/records will add evidence to my arguments?

At this point you will need to assess if the materials you have gathered are enough to enable you to answer your intended exam questions in sufficient depth and breadth.

Exam essays share characteristics found in coursework essays and other assignments, so the criteria highlighted on the marking guide for your coursework assignments will indicate some targets to aim for in your exam answers. However, there is another source of guidance that is especially focused and useful, but is frequently overlooked by students. It can be summed up in the following piece of advice:

Don't forget what your tutors have said!

You can use the feedback you have gained from past assignments as a guide to help you judge just how deeply you may need to delve into your subject in terms of exam preparation. Do you need to 'beef up' your analysis, the sorts of argument you need to present or the range of subject matter you need to include? Your revision strategy should aim to incorporate any strengths that your tutors have identified in previous work, as well as rectifying any weaknesses they have specifically commented on. Having taken these into account, you may need to do some additional reading to fill in the gaps in your notes and/or think more deeply about the significance of the material you already have.

Practice makes perfect!

Exams essentially test a person's ability to *perform* a certain task on a given day. So, a final, indispensable step in the revision process is to *practise* this performance by writing your own 'mock' answers under exam conditions. There is a lot to be learned by taking revision materials and using them to write answers to past exam questions. Most importantly, it forces you to consider which parts of your revision material are most valuable in helping you to answer the questions central to any given topic. You also get practice in *linking* the revision material, arranging it into an unfolding, logical argument. All of these processes are central to the writing of good exam essays.

Having organised your revision materials on a topic, attempt to write essay plans, or even whole exam answers, under timed conditions, without looking again at your notes. Writing out your answer applies to 'seen' papers, too; you can determine if you can present your written argument within the given time frame. The more one practises the performance of writing exam answers, under exam conditions, the less intimidating it becomes.

Organising your study schedule

Revising material for exams is undoubtedly an arduous activity that requires from a person a good deal of personal commitment and mental effort. Nevertheless, there are things you can do to make the whole business more manageable.

Having worked out how much time you need to devote to each topic of study, you need to identify the times in the day when you are most alert. Plan to do the most intellectually demanding aspects of your revision during those times. Other, less challenging activities, such as organising notes, following up references or updating your study timetable, can be fitted in during those periods when your concentration is less.

Making revision manageable

Aim to keep your revision periods short and focused, with regular breaks for refreshment and recreation. Set yourself specific, realistic tasks for each study session. Name them in words and write them down, big and bold, so you don't forget.

It is much more likely that you will achieve a specific goal such as 'Between 9 and 11 a.m. today I will read and make notes on chapter 4'. than if you vaguely decide to 'Read about Vygotsky on Thursday'. Specific goals = Achievable results.

Break up long study sessions into periods of no more than forty-five minutes of revision, followed by a five-minute break. Use the remaining ten minutes of the hour to *review* what you have just looked at, reflecting on what you have learned, and summing it up briefly in your own words. This should allow you to judge, at the end of each hour, how much of the revision material is actually being understood and remembered. There is no point in ploughing through material from dawn till dusk if nothing is going in!

Take a short break of at least fifteen minutes between each hourly session, to relax and process what you have learned before starting again. After three hours of study you will need, and deserve, a longer break to recharge your batteries. It is normally much more productive to revise more than one subject per day, as your mind will benefit from the variety in encountering different material. Study a different subject in the afternoon from the one you studied in the morning. 'A change is as good as a rest' applies as much to revision as to other activities in life.

Try to make the whole process as enjoyable as possible by building in appropriate treats and rewards, at regular intervals, to keep you going. If any negative thoughts creep into your mind, try visualising successfully answering the questions on the exam paper, reminding yourself of all the benefits that such success will bring for you personally.

Remember, it's not just your head that you will be taking into the exam room – look after your whole self. Try to get eight hours of sleep a night, eat a healthy diet, avoid too many stimulants and drink lots of water. Take regular, reasonable breaks for exercise and to meet up with friends. This should ensure that you are in the best condition to give your utmost on the day of the exam itself.

How do I memorise what I have learned?

For some students, memorising material for exams presents a problem. By far the best aid to memory is ensuring that, when you look at your revision notes, you can answer the questions: 'What, in simple terms, do my notes mean?' and 'How do they help me to answer the key questions regarding this subject?' Understanding the *basics* of your topic, rather than being able to use fancy language or remember long quotations, is the best way to ensure that you can say something meaningful about it in an exam. If your poor memory is because of a disability, then discuss this with your tutor or disability advisor so that you can access any available support.

Memory and the multi-sensory mind

Many students find that the very process of distilling their notes into brief bullet-point summaries helps them to understand the material and how it can be organised into a logical sequence to answer a question. However, the human brain tends to remember material that it has encountered through a number of senses, as shown below.

HANDY HINT

How we remember things

Tests have indicated that we remember:

- 20% of what we read
- 30% of what we hear
- 40% of what we see
- 50% of what we say
- 60% of what we do

and **90%** of what we **read, hear, say and do!**

Source: Adapted from research by Edgar Dale in the 1960s and his 'Cone of Learning'.

Try to vary your revision technique by making it as *multi-sensory* as possible. Making colourful mind maps or posters of topic outlines, audio-recording lists and essay plans or even videoing a conversation about a topic with friends – all these should increase your likelihood of remembering revision material over an extended period of time. And it goes without saying that the more times you look at, rehearse and try to link in this material to what you already know about a topic, the less likely you are to forget it on the day of the exam itself.

Revision strategies

Consider whether your revision strategy has included the following:

Have I:	**Yes**	**No**
looked at past essay papers for the last three or more years?		
identified recurring questions/common themes in these papers?		
related these 'core' questions to my essays/lecture notes and reading throughout the term/academic year?		
identified where I need to add to my revision materials by extra reading or reflection on key issues raised by past exam questions?		
written outlines/essay skeletons in point form, together with brief references that summarise my exam answers in a memorable way?		
practised writing exam answers under exam conditions and analysed the strengths and weaknesses of my answers?		
tested myself to see if I can remember these outlines without any aids?		

What to do in the exam

Having prepared well using the techniques suggested, you should be reasonably confident by the time you enter the exam room. However, there are ways to help you reduce your anxiety level and maximise your chances of success in the exam.

First, having clearly identified *where* and *when* the exam is taking place, plan to arrive at the exam room with plenty of time to spare, making allowances for any possible delays. It is important that you maintain a calm and balanced state of mind. Try to avoid stressful situations: find a quiet corner and thumb through the bullet points and reference material on your revision memory cards to help you maintain control.

Make sure that you have a good supply of pens, an eraser, a ruler, a watch that works and can be clearly read and any other equipment that you are allowed to take into the exam itself. Don't forget to take some water and something to stave off hunger pangs. Maintaining your blood sugar levels is important to your ability to concentrate.

Reading the exam paper

When you receive the exam paper, read through the instructions, and also listen to any instructions given by the invigilator *very carefully*. Use this as an opportunity to calm yourself down and maintain a relaxed mental state. Read through *all* of the exam questions very carefully, ticking off the ones that you feel you have a good chance of answering. Then read through them again *slowly and deliberately*, double ticking the ones that you feel you can answer best. Making the best choice of questions will maximise your chances of doing well. It is surprising how many students rush this stage, and so fail to make the best choice of questions for the information they have learned.

Once you have chosen your question to answer, *read it through twice*, carefully and deliberately, underlining each important word or key term. This should ensure that you interpret the question accurately, identifying the main focus of the question and its most important components. Having done this, you should attempt to make a brief essay plan (in bullet points or mind map form), noting down any reference material (names, dates, theories, legislation, quotations, workplace experience) while they are still fresh in your mind.

Don't worry if this takes up to 20 per cent of the time allocated for that question. Such careful planning should ensure that your work is much more likely to answer the question and do so in a logical, structured way – important features that examiners look for in exam answers.

Timing and answering the questions successfully

If each question on the exam paper attracts an equal number of marks, you should try to give the same amount of time to answering each question. Write out the start and finish times for each question where you can clearly see them – it is very easy to lose track of time when you are under pressure.

If you do run out of time to complete a question, and have a lot more to say, leave some space and briefly conclude your answer, noting down any additional material in point form, in the spaces left. Not only might you gain some marks by indicating what you would have included, you may also have an opportunity to go back and develop those points in a more complete way at the end of the exam.

Try to plan for some time, perhaps five minutes or so, at the end of each question to review what you have written, making necessary additions or changes. If you write on every other line of the answer paper (essentially double spacing your writing) you should find this editing much easier. Double spacing may make your whole paper easier for the examiner to read – especially if your handwriting is on the large or shaky side!

If you find that, having answered all of your questions, there is still time remaining, use that time to look over the answers you have written, rather than leaving the exam room early. Most pieces of work can be improved by a little thoughtful re-reading, followed by some sensitive minor reworking. Introductions and conclusions make a particularly strong impression on the reader, so it is well worth devoting any spare minutes at the end of your exam to making minor changes that improve the balance and impact of your answer.

Surviving the exam

Finally, once the exam is over, try to banish it from your mind and resist the temptation to indulge in 'what ifs'. It is notoriously difficult to judge your own exam performance, and rarely worth expending the mental stamina to do so. If there is anything you have learned that will benefit your next exam, by all means use that knowledge constructively. Otherwise, save your energy for any further revision you have to do. Rather than 'beating yourself up', visualise how you will celebrate your success and freedom once the exams are over and you have earned a really good rest!

Having read about exam techniques in this chapter, now ask yourself the following questions:

- Are there any good things in my past revision approach that I should keep and build on?
- Are there any things that have let me down in the past that need changing?
- What do I need to change *most* about my revision and what should I do to make a start?
- When should I start making those changes?
- Is there anything stopping me from revising each day as I learn my subject?

Searching for information

Chapter 2 considers basic search strategies, but finding appropriate and relevant sources of information for study can be a challenge. The range of sources available is varied: government documents, books, information gateways, websites, databases and, of course, the media is an ever-expanding source of information. So, whether you are working towards writing an essay, case study, examination or any other form of assessment activity, time invested in developing good search strategies is time well spent.

Developing key word search strategies

When searching for resources students often complain of two problems; one is of being overwhelmed by the amount of resources found and the other is of not being able to find anything! Both problems can be minimised by effective search methods.

The physical search for reading resources, whether in a library or online, is best tackled after you have prepared a list of key words to help you in your search. This is important for several reasons; it allows time to think about the vocabulary of the subject under scrutiny and consider alternative words and phrases that could be used in a search, and it provides the opportunity to consider expert authors in the field, which can save time when searching. A mind map or spider diagram can be the starting place for such a search, or, if you prefer, you can make a linear list of words. For example, if your assignment/essay requires 'A case study of one or two children or young people with an analysis of one or more factors that affect their learning', you might start by considering all the possible factors that affect learning. These might include some of the factors listed below.

Factors affecting learning

- Cognitive ability – including learning disability
- Health – food and nutrition
- Family situation/education of parents
- Motivation and willingness to learn
- Self-confidence/self-esteem
- Gender
- Classroom expectations and behaviour strategies
- Feelings of safety and security
- Social interactions and peer pressures
- School structure and strategies
- Learning and teaching styles
- Age

From this list you might select one factor that affects learning related to your study group. From this selection you can then begin to create a key word search list. For example, if the case study is based upon a boy and a girl of similar age and ability but whose attainment is unequal, then 'gender' might be a factor worth investigating. A key word search list might include as many variations as possible of words and phrases around this topic, e.g. boys' attainment, boys' attainment in education (or literacy or maths), boys' behaviour, boys' behavior, academic achievement, girls' attainment, pupil attainment, gender differences, sex differences, gender attitudes in learning, school attitudes, boys' culture, 12-year-old boys, etc. The more variations you have, including American spellings, the more likely you are to find something of value for your study.

Search engines and databases

Key words can be used to search for information through library catalogues, online search facilities or through online databases. A search engine locates relevant sources very quickly, matching key words to the contents of its database. One of the most common search engines, Google, will find over 12,000,000 matches for 'boys' attainment in education' in less than thirty seconds – presenting a problem because of the large number of 'hits'! It will be necessary to refine the search so as to reduce the potential number of sources and ensure that the most relevant and appropriate sources are located.

Google has a specialised academic section, Google Scholar, which narrows the hits using the same search words to 140,000 results. Changing search engines to the Education Resources Information Centre (ERIC) database finds 315 matches for 'boys' attainment in education'. This is a more manageable number and these sources are likely to be more relevant than the ones found by a general search of Google. ERIC (www.eric.ed.gov) claims to have the 'world's largest digital library of education literature', mainly made up of journal articles, and is one of a number of academic databases that students become familiar with during their studies. (Others are listed at the end of this chapter.) The advantage of using an 'academic' search engine or database is that the contents have already been selected for academic merit and are more reliable as sources of information than are some of the other sources floating around in cyberspace.

Searching for information using any database or search engine is relatively simple, and many have built-in search options, giving the chance to narrow a search by key words, date of publication or other parameters. This is invaluable, particularly when a search turns up a large number of results. Most database searches are based upon what is known as implied 'Boolean logic', and understanding how this works may help you to understand the results of your key word searches.

Using Boolean logic

Boolean logic is a form of algebraic logic based upon the two opposing ideas of *true* and *false*, and named after the mathematician George Boole (*An Investigation of the Laws of Thought*, published in 1854). His 'logic' is used when searching databases by using Boolean 'operators' (AND, OR and NOT) together with key words to expand or narrow searches. This is best explained through the use of Venn diagrams. For example, the greyed areas in Figures 8.1 and 8.2 indicate what is retrieved when the words OR and AND are inserted between two key words.

Using the Boolean operators AND and OR with additional key words in the search box will continue to broaden or narrow your search, as shown in Figure 8.3.

Using this pattern and combining key words in this way can make any search more efficient. The operators can be used simply, as shown above, or you can include a number of your key words in more complex combinations. For example, consider the combination in Figure 8.4.

Notice the use of brackets to group key words together, and that the Boolean operators are typed in capital letters. Following this method when searching, even

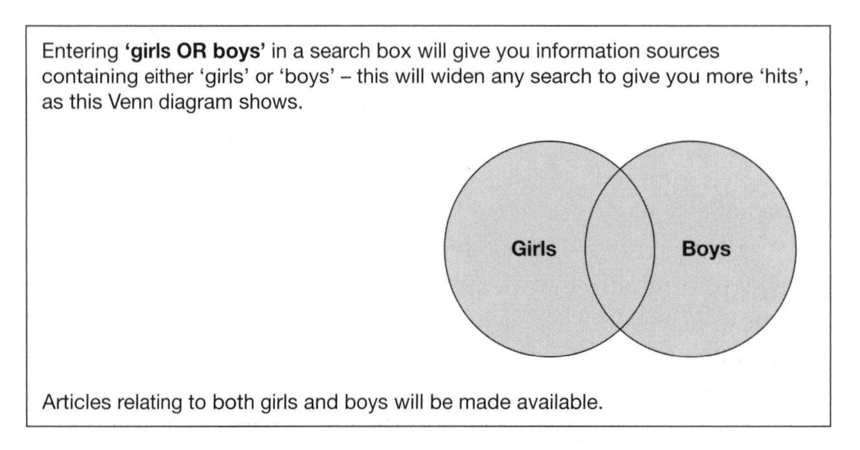

Figure 8.1 Using the Boolean OR operator

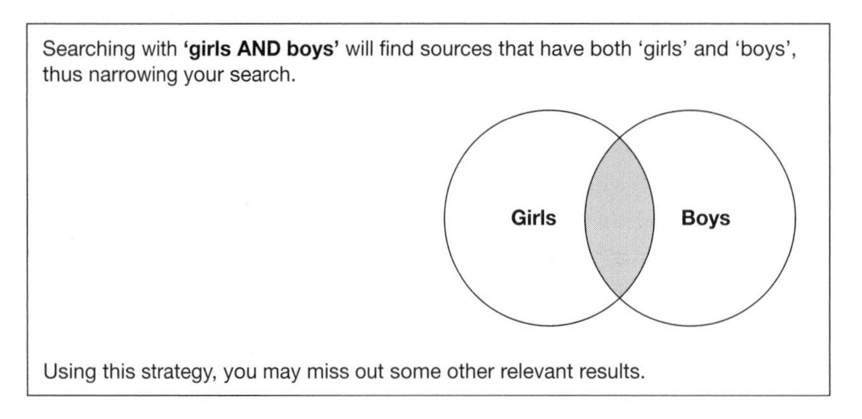

Figure 8.2 Using the Boolean AND operator

Searching with **'girls AND boys AND attainment'** will find articles and sources that have 'girls', 'boys' and 'attainment', thus narrowing your search further.

Using this strategy, you may miss out some other relevant results.

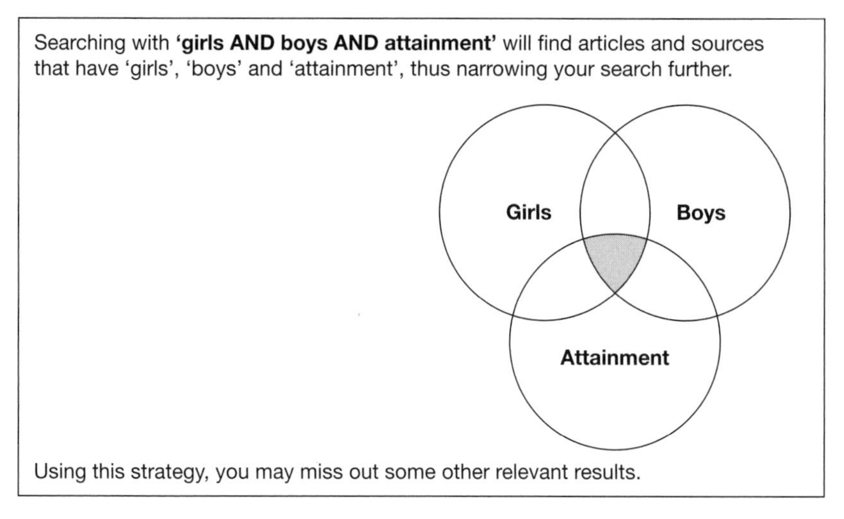

Figure 8.3 Using the AND operator and an additional key word

(boys AND girls) AND (attainment OR academic achievement) AND (UK OR England)

Figure 8.4 A complex search combining AND and OR operators

when using a large search engine such as Google, is more likely to return relevant and appropriate resources.

The last Boolean logic operator is NOT, which will exclude items from your search parameters, although it is not used as frequently as AND and OR because it is not as effective. For example, to exclude all articles that referred to girls and girls' attainment, then the Boolean search string might read as in Figure 8.5.

(boys NOT girls) AND (attainment OR achievement)

Figure 8.5 Using the Boolean NOT operator in a search

Understanding the basics of Boolean logic will give you some insight into how many of the common databases and search engines locate sources. However, most common search engines/databases offer built-in methods of searching without the need for full use of Boolean logic operators. You will be able to spot how this works when you enter more than one key word and the search engine offers suggestions to guide your search. For example, Google offers the suggestions shown in Figure 8.6 when you type 'boys attain' in the search box. And when you enter 'boys and girls attainment', further suggestions to help with the search are offered (Figure 8.7).

These suggestions may offer some support in finding sources, but it is always worth remembering that any database is part of a machine, and however helpful and useful it is, you will only get out of it what is put in! You need to select your key words yourself in order to find the most relevant resources, rather than rely on the search engine. As in all things, the more skilled and expert you are, the more effective and efficient you will become.

Learning to use the searching facilities of the various academic databases listed at the end of this chapter will support your independent studies and offer a wider choice of reading matter. Do not rely upon one database, but broaden the scope of your studies so as to embrace a wider range of sources.

boys attain

boys attain**ment in education**
boys attain**ment**
boys attain**ment in literacy**
boys attain**ment in writing**

Figure 8.6 Search suggestions in the Google search interface

boys and girls attainment

boys and girls attainment
determinants of school attainment **of** boys and girls **in turkey**
investigating the patterns of differential attainment **of** boys and girls
accounting for the differential attainment **of** boys and girls **at school**

Figure 8.7 Another example of Google search suggestions

Recording your searches

It is important to record any searches so that you can find the sources again. Keeping a bibliography of all the books/e-sources that you find is essential, even the books or sites that you 'reject', but how you do this will be up to you. You can simply keep a notebook and jot down the reference details alongside your notes, or keep an e-copy of the bibliography; this has an advantage in that you can later copy and paste the bibliographical entry into your assessed work.

When you borrow books from the library you will generate a library loan history, which is useful because you can check it to see what you have read. This may help if you have a hazy memory of a text that you need to refer to again and cannot remember exactly what it was! When you are working in the library, you could photocopy the title page of each book you are browsing and add to the copy any copyright information (such as publisher and date), thus ensuring that you have a record of the information required for a bibliographic entry. Then use the reverse side of the photocopy to make your initial notes when reading. The page can then be placed in a ring binder, providing you with a visual image of the books that you have read as well as keeping relevant notes together.

The most challenging search records to keep often relate to online searches, as it is so easy to reject a web page or e-journal article, only to want to check it again and find that it has gone! One way around this is to ensure that as you search you copy and paste the relevant URLs into a dated document that you will file at the end of your search. Adding a selected e-journal article or government web page into your 'favourites' or 'bookmarks' may also help you to locate the source at a later date. Be sure, however, to organise the folders in your favourites/bookmarks carefully!

Summary

This chapter has addressed the question of why exams are set, and their importance as a means of assessing students' intellectual development. It has also suggested some ways in which to make sensible predictions regarding future exam questions and how to develop effective revision techniques that make the most of the limited time and resources available.

Undoubtedly, the best way to remember any given piece of knowledge is to become actively engaged with your studies. In the final analysis, enjoying your subject and being motivated to learn for its own sake is possibly the most powerful factor in doing well in any sphere of activity. Developing search skills and strategies can enhance your learning and study as well as provide you with relevant, reliable and appropriate reading resources for assignments and assessment tasks.

Learn to appreciate what you are studying, determining and deciding your success criteria, and make these your goals. This will ensure that you achieve your best from adult learning, whether in coursework or in examinations.

Further reading

There are many textbooks and online resources aimed at being successful in examinations and overcoming exam nerves. Consider searching for the work of the following authors:

Lucinda Becker
Stella Cottrell
Phil Davies
Patrick McMurray
Tony Buzan
Dr Hiten Vyas

Matthew M. Thomas
Mel Trudgett.

Many university websites offer tips on exams; 'search' their websites using key words. Here are just two to consider:

1. Open University – revision and examination guides covering a range of topics, including stress and revision, available at http://www2.open.ac.uk/students/skillsforstudy/.
2. Hull University – 'How to survive exams' leaflet, currently available at http://www2.hull.ac.uk/student/pdf/dysrevsurvive.pdf.

Databases and search engines

The following are some databases and search engines in common use:

- ERIC – Education Resources Information Centre (www.eric.ed.gov)
- BEI – British Education Index Free Collections (Education-line) (www.leeds.ac.uk/bei/)
- DfE – Department for Education (www.education.gov.uk)
- EEP – Educational Evidence Portal (www.eep.ac.uk)
- BASE – Bielefeld Academic Search Engine (http://www.base-search.net/)
- Google Scholar – part of the most popular search engine in common use (http://scholar.google.co.uk/)
- Refseek – an academic search engine (http://www.refseek.com/).

9 Reflection, reassurance and relaxation!

Introduction

This chapter takes a last look at the challenges facing you when you embark on an academic programme. In some ways it repeats and expands upon some of the ideas contained in the previous chapters, to serve as a quick reminder and reference. The chapter also considers some techniques to raise performance and confidence that may be helpful to you. In all, it hopes to offer more support for the 3Rs – reflection, reassurance and relaxation. The chapter opens by considering the way tutors mark work and the academically important area of critical reflection.

Reflecting upon learning and practice

Considering the marking criteria

Academic writing is a style of writing that is phrased more carefully, precisely and accurately than everyday speech or writing. It is considered more 'scientific' than some other forms of writing, in that it should be formal and logically structured and sequenced. Academic writing also makes a clear distinction between facts and opinions, and these are supported with evidence through reference to research and reading. It is also more tentative in its conclusions – showing awareness that there may be possible arguments or evidence yet to emerge. These components of academic style will be incorporated into your assignment marking criteria, which will also contain detailed descriptions of the different levels of competence that correspond to the different marking grades. These will range from a fail to a distinction (or F to A grade). Tutors use the marking criteria to award grades, but they require evidence of your competence level to be demonstrated in your assignment/essay before they can accurately grade your work. So, for example, even if you have read many books on a subject in preparation for your writing, but fail to reference these in your work you cannot be given credit for that reading. It becomes your responsibility as a student to ensure that you provide evidence to meet the assessment criteria, so that tutors are able to grade your assignment. For some aspects of academic writing this may be fairly straightforward and easily learnt. Look at the basic list of assessment criteria below and compare this model with the marking policy of your own course.

Example of basic criteria that tutors may use to mark work

Basic criteria	Evidence will include
Knowledge and understanding	■ Reference to relevant reading ■ A demonstration of the awareness of key authors/ researchers ■ Ability to link theory with practice
Views and arguments	■ Ability to express views and arguments clearly ■ An awareness of the range of views and opinions surrounding the topic ■ Ability to use relevant evidence to support personal views and the views of others
Analysis and reflection	■ Ability to reflect upon concepts and key ideas ■ Demonstration of an awareness of the significance of research and evidence ■ An ability to draw sound and meaningful conclusions from reading and experiences
Expression	■ Ability to write clearly, accurately and correctly ■ Demonstration of an awareness of academic conventions in writing style ■ Ability to select appropriate texts and use them to support arguments
Organisation	■ Logically structured work ■ All references and bibliographical details correctly set out ■ Well-presented work, either word-processed or hand-written in an acceptable format

Hopefully, you will now be aware of the accepted structures (organisation), expression and referencing (knowledge and understanding) required within academic writing – three of the items from the marking guide. These rules are easily learnt and followed, or at least a book such as this will help you ensure that your work is organised well, correctly referenced, etc. 'Views and arguments' is perhaps slightly more problematic, but if you have planned your work well during the initial stages you will know what the main aim, or argument, of your work is going to be, and then collect the views and opinions of others (as well as your own) through reading to develop and support your stance. What is arguably harder to demonstrate in the initial stages of academic work is the ability to analyse and reflect. 'Your work is too descriptive, be more reflective', is a common feedback comment from tutors.

What do tutors look for when marking?

Tutors generally use the language of the marking grid in their feedback, so you should be able to determine where you are in relation to each strand by studying the criteria and matching this with the tutor's feedback. Below is a chart of the main strands used when marking assignments. Look at the chart and then consider the

The main strands used in marking assignments

Strand	**Evidence will include**
Knowledge (and understanding)	Relevant reading, bibliography, depth of insight and understanding
Views and arguments	Views expressed, balance of views given, evidence used to support argument (reading and workplace), argument developed, some awareness of the limitations of research
Analysis (and reflection)	Not descriptive! Questioning of assumptions and awareness of the significance of evidence, with sound, relevant conclusions drawn
Expression	Comprehensible, formal vocabulary (no colloquialisms), issues discussed clearly, accurate grammar, punctuation and spelling
Organisation	Clear structure, with introduction, clearly sequenced argument with each paragraph related logically to the others, and leading through to a linked conclusion.

three paragraphs in Figures 9.1 to 9.3. Use the strands to find evidence within the paragraph to 'mark' the work. Indicate with a tick each time you find evidence in the paragraphs that matches the criteria. What problems can you find?

Please note that it is advisable to use the full marking grid from your institution to understand the progression of each strand when you examine your own work. In the three paragraphs used here, the referenced works are fictitious!

Examples of just one paragraph in length would not be sufficient to mark a whole assignment, but consider how each of the paragraphs illustrated gives a 'flavour' of

The NC orders for the English curriculum say that English is divided into three parts: Speaking and Listening, Reading and Writing. In my school the teachers teach English through the use of a story book. The children sit on the carpet area and the teacher reads the book picked out from a book list. As she reads the book she gets the children to look out for sound patterns and to chat about the different characters in the book. The children are encouraged to ask questions by putting up their hands or using the 'traffic light' cards and the teacher does ask lots of questions. The questions are often about the characters and many of them are closed questions, which I don't think are very good for making the children think. However, sometimes open questions are asked so that the children have to think about what the story is about.

Knowledge?	Views?	Analysis?	Expression?

Figure 9.1 Assignment writing – paragraph 1

My school bases its English teaching on story books as this offers a strategy for delivering the Foundation Stage and National Curriculum (1989) targets that I believe is very effective. The books used are carefully chosen by the teacher to interest the children. I think that this supports the ideas of Martin Green that children learn book language through listening to stories in Martin Green's *Listening to Stories* (published by Friends Publications in 2010). This motivates the children so that they are ready to listen to the story as they gather on the carpet area. The children always show good listening behaviours. The teacher points out key words and the children respond to the sound patterns showing how much they know. I also think that the games the teacher introduces for the children during this time make the learning fun and therefore more memorable. They show this by readily joining in and by their quick recall of the sounds previously learned when questioned by the teacher.

Knowledge?	Views?	Analysis?	Expression?

Figure 9.2 Assignment writing – paragraph 2

Within my workplace, story reading is used to promote learning through a range of teaching strategies. The discursive and interactive nature when sharing stories on the carpet area seems to motivate children to learn (Green, 2010, p. 63). As Brown (2011, p. 16) also indicates, reading is an important life skill but the sharing of text 'involves children in social activities and thinking skills that expands their knowledge and understanding'. Furthermore, Brown suggests that when young children are encouraged to listen and share books together they are more likely to engage in reading themselves for pleasure (Brown, 2011, p. 45). Creating an atmosphere of social intimacy by gathering on the carpet area to share a story together, carefully structuring questions that allow children to discuss the plot and characters will therefore go some way to building a love of reading that is essential for promoting future readers.

Knowledge?	Views?	Analysis?	Expression?

Figure 9.3 Assignment writing – paragraph 3

the whole. You could pause here and try to write a fourth, improved paragraph, or take just one of the paragraphs from a piece of your own work and 'mark' it using the same criteria.

The reflective element: moving towards critical analysis

Reflection is an important part of learning, and is part of the process that allows learners to move on to the next stage in learning. Reflection may be thought of as looking in a mirror and beginning to ask questions about what you see; it is a time to pause and look carefully at the image. You may be aware of the increase of thinking and questioning skills being employed in the classroom, as ways of encouraging reflection and therefore 'deep-level learning', as opposed to 'surface learning', which is quickly forgotten. One of the main purposes of reflection is to consolidate learning. We probably all mentally reflect on our experiences and learning activities, but to show this in academic writing may require some thought. Initially, if you pause during your writing and ask yourself the following three basic questions, and incorporate the answers into your writing, then evidence of reflection will begin to emerge:

1. What have I done?
2. What have I learned (about myself, children, theories, etc.)?
3. What difference to the future will this make?

The first question is often where new writers stop. If you answer only this question your work will be descriptive, even if the answer is related to reading.

However, if you go on to consider the significance of what you have found out, preferably from a range of sources, this is evidence of reflection. Take this further and discuss how what you have found out informs new practice, and either changes or confirms your thinking. Then your writing will begin to demonstrate evidence of critical reflection and analysis. By consciously including the main strands of your thinking in your writing as you read and study, you can make your tutor aware of the critical reflective process in which you are engaging as you learn, and of the subtle changes that take place as you notice and relate to new ideas. Assignments and essays that reach the distinction level in marking generally contain strong evidence of critical reflection, as well as being logically structured, well supported by evidence and academically expressed.

Writing that just gives information or records an event or situation will be perceived as 'descriptive' by academic tutors. This may demonstrate some 'knowledge' but offers little in the way of 'understanding'. In the same way, offering long quotations from reading in your assignments gives an indication of what you have read, but does not show that you have understood what you have read. It is far better, therefore, to avoid too many quotations in your written work and to paraphrase instead, remembering to acknowledge the source of the information through accurate referencing. This will indicate that you are analysing and interpreting the information that you are reading. In the same way, offering your thinking and interpretation when recording workplace events and observations will make your work more analytical and less descriptive. Usually, this can be included in an organised way, for example, by first recording the workplace event/observation in a descriptive way and then adding a reflective commentary. This commentary could include your thinking, as well as reference to reading or research, and demonstrate clearly your developing academic abilities. Even if workplace tasks are not formally marked in the same way as assignments, the practice of being analytical in this way will develop your skills.

Breaking through the stress barriers

Change is one of the certainties of life, as new ideas replace the old, and new people join the workplace as others leave, and so on. Change in status, career, home and even physical appearance (have you ever been on a diet, or changed your hairstyle?) is dreamt of and planned for by many people. Personal stress and uncertainty are often an accepted part of that change. When you change because you want to, the temporary stress induced by the change becomes a minor inconvenience and part of the drive to move forward to achieve success. However, some stress associated with change inhibits achievement and can prevent the change from taking place. Nearly everyone feels nervous as they begin to study for a degree, but some people admit to greater feelings of anxiety and stress than others. This may make those people feel uncomfortable and prevent them from making the most of what is on offer.

When you are out of your 'comfort zone', that is, the situations, events and places where you feel in control and know that you can cope, then you may begin to feel the physical effects of stress. These physical side-effects, such as blushing, sweating, feelings of tightness or even of blind panic, can prevent you from taking a full part in the proceedings and even inhibit learning. Each person's comfort zone is different – for example, some people readily become leaders of the group, and others prefer to be followers; some people enjoy speaking in public whereas others would much rather stay quiet. If you are just outside of your comfort zone you may be excited or challenged, corresponding to a state of tension. However, if you experience blushing, sweating or other physical feelings that make you feel as if you must escape, then you are heading towards your panic zone.

To get some idea of where your comfort zones extend, consider the situations in the table below and decide where you fit in relation to them.

Considering your comfort zones – what causes you stress?

Think about all the aspects of the following situations and imagine 'being there'. How does it feel?

Situation	**Which zone would this place you in?**		
	Comfort zone	Tension zone	Panic zone
Reading a story to a class of children			
Giving a 15-minute presentation to other students			
Attending an interview for a new job			
Writing a 4000-word essay			
Having coffee with friends			
Talking to your head teacher/employer			
Singing in public (karaoke?)			
Making a point in group discussion			
Preparing lunch for 10 guests			

The extreme feelings caused by being out of a comfort zone may explain phobias, the seemingly irrational emotions that some people experience when they see a spider, or board an aeroplane. These may be so severe that they prevent the person from doing what they want to do, such as going on holiday. However, most people have the ability to extend their own comfort zones by learning to do things that once might have seemed impossible. The majority of fears can be overcome by gradually facing the fear and learning to live with it, and so becoming more comfortable and reducing feelings of stress. By deliberately extending your comfort zones and consciously enjoying the successful outcomes, you can prove to yourself that you can change and therefore be successful the next time. By believing that you can be successful in what you set out to do, you extend your comfort zone and thus reduce the feelings of stress.

Performance and self-talk

Linked to the idea of extending comfort zones is the notion of self-talk. This is the inner conversation that everyone has with themselves which can have a direct bearing on each individual's performance. 'Performance' in this sense describes the way people behave in any given situation; for example, people may be kind, friendly, argumentative, creative or even clever. People perform in this way without thinking about it because it is part of their self-image – it's just the way they are! Most people are happy with the way they perform, but sometimes also wish to be able to change – to feel more confident when speaking in public, or to become more creative or less argumentative. To do this successfully you have to change the way you think about yourself – you have to change your self-image. Often, this self-image has been created from the way others close to you have talked to you and about you from childhood, particularly if you have accepted their view as being correct. This is why children should never be called 'stupid' or 'naughty', as they may come to believe this judgement and behave in accordance with that belief. It then becomes difficult to change the way an individual behaves, because the behaviour becomes a habit.

One way to change self-image is to listen to the inner conversation that you have with yourself, and if the talk is negative change the talk to positive. The way you think about yourself strongly determines the way you will behave in the future. This becomes a cycle, in that everyone behaves in the way in which they think they should behave, unconsciously and with little variation. If you believe that you are scared of spiders, when you see a spider you will be scared! Similarly, if you believe that you have never been good at writing academically, then you will not be able to write academically! Self-belief is very powerful! Try checking some of your beliefs about your self-image by reading these statements aloud, slowly. Which statements feel 'right'?

- I am a non-smoker/I am a smoker.
- I am overweight/I am physically fit.

- I am successful at study/I am not academic.
- I am popular with my peers/I am respected by everyone I meet.

It is possible to lie to yourself, but difficult – people generally feel uncomfortable when they lie. So, if you are telling yourself the truth, then that is what you are and that indicates how you will be in the future. If you acknowledge that you are a smoker and then try to give up cigarettes, you will find this difficult because, deep down, you know that you are still a smoker. Your whole being will want to conform to your belief. One way to change your performance, to become a non-smoker, is to change your belief. You can try to do this by consciously changing your self-talk.

You can begin to change the way you behave by consciously controlling some of the thoughts about who and what you are. You can extend your comfort zones by concentrating on the positive outcomes of the things that you do, rather than focusing on the negative. When you do things well, listen to the inner voice! As friends and colleagues and tutors give you praise for tasks done well, check that your *inner* voice, your self-talk, says 'Yes, I did do that well', even if your public voice is more modest! You may resist this, as most people find that mistakes and public failures occupy most of their thinking time, pushing out successes from their conscious thought. Learn from the mistakes that you make, but do not dwell on them. Instead, create successful belief in yourself by consciously spending more time thinking about your successes than about your failures. Mentally noting the times when you perform well at everyday activities and the behaviours that you want to strengthen will help to build resilience to failure and promote success.

Within the classroom, you may also have noticed that children can be encouraged to behave well if adults praise and acknowledge those behaviours that they want. It is thought that for every reprimand given, a child needs a further twenty words of praise to overcome the negative feelings generated by the reprimand. This works for adults too, but it is rare to receive praise from others, so adults need to award the praise to themselves! So, target the areas in which you wish to change your performance and give yourself lots of congratulations as you succeed in moving towards your goal. For example, if you wish to engage more in group or class discussion, each time you contribute during a session, make sure that you mentally acknowledge your success and congratulate yourself. Tell yourself that it is just the way you are – a good communicator and contributor. You will not extend your comfort zone overnight, but you should steadily gain confidence until your self-image allows you to contribute to discussion naturally and without any feelings of stress.

Recording success is also a powerful motivator and can build confidence. This is where action planning and monitoring becomes important. Visit your action plans and note even the small signs of success, as this will pull you even closer to your goals. Surprisingly, feelings of stress may be present when you are successful, or performing in a way that is 'too good' for you. Sometimes, you may hear yourself say things to yourself like 'that must be wrong, I don't usually do so well', and the next time you try the same thing you might struggle to repeat previous success. If you behave in a way contrary to your current self-image, it causes stress; this is being out of your comfort zone in a different way, and can also be explained by the idea of self-talk.

Each person learns and thinks in different ways, so other techniques may also help you to achieve success. If you have panic attacks at the thought of writing assignments, giving presentations or taking exams, try out some of the techniques below to help you to overcome these feelings and barriers to performance; but, as Henry Ford reputedly once said, 'Whether you think you can or you can't – you're right!'

Removing performance barriers

Test the following techniques to see if they will help you. You will find that if you use these techniques often, with practice you will get better at removing the barriers and feeling calm and more in control.

Take a step back and become detached from the problem	If you find that you are feeling stressed or worried, you may find yourself becoming controlled by the emotion that is generated. Become detached and calmer by doing the following: 1 Think of a past experience when you felt stressed or had strong negative feelings. 2 Imagine that you put those feelings in a box and throw the box away. 3 Imagine how it feels now that you are no longer anxious or stressed by the feelings, and how you control your own actions and behaviour. Enjoy the feelings of being in control and rational about past problems, and transfer these feelings to the new stress factors. Tell yourself that you are bigger than the problem and the stress will not control you! If you fail at something (as everyone does at some time!) tell yourself: 'I made a mistake there, but I am learning from the mistake. The NEXT time I do that I shall do it well, without mistakes.'

Remind yourself that you can do it!	An affirmation is a statement of fact. However, people generally repeat to themselves more negative statements than positive ones, for example, 'I can't do that!' is probably something you think to yourself rather than 'I am good at that!'. Creating and using positive affirmations can help you to feel better when facing difficult situations. 1 First identify what your goal behaviour is (perhaps to feel more confident when speaking during discussion). 2 Create a short personal sentence about yourself (writing this down will make it more powerful and help you to remember it). 3 The sentence should be personal, positive, in the present tense and have some emotion attached to it. 4 Enjoy reading the sentence to yourself at least once a day! For example, an affirmation might read: 'I feel confident in discussions and enjoy debates with other students.' Follow this by noting your successes in discussions (even small ones) and congratulating yourself.
Work at supporting other students and having shared goals	If you talk with other students you will probably find that you all feel apprehensive about the course, study or assignments. Work together to help each other towards your common goal of success. If you pull together and help each other you may find that being part of a group gives you the strength to face the difficult times without giving up.
Relaxation and mental imagery	Sit quietly and relax – start by thinking about your feet and how heavy they are, and gradually work up your body until all your muscles feel relaxed. Now think of something that you have been successful at. Picture it, smell it, and even touch it, if you can, in your mind. Now create a mental picture of what you want to be able to do. Imagine yourself reaching your goal, listening to the praise of success and even smelling the success. Link this to some previous success you have enjoyed. Enjoy the feelings of success and feel pleased with yourself. Practise this regularly to project positive images of your success into the future. Know that you are going to be successful in what you set out to do.

Catch yourself being good at things	Whenever you catch yourself doing the right thing, contributing to discussion, learning a new concept, take a bit of time to enjoy the feelings of success and to congratulate yourself. It is possible that you spend more time mentally telling yourself what you do wrong, rather than you do in celebrating what you do right. Spend some time mentally rehearsing the good performances and dismiss the poor performances by saying 'That's not like me, the next time I will perform at a much higher level.' Do this silently, as most people will be put off if you start telling them how good you are! This can be a useful technique to raise self-esteem and help to build up resilience to overcome failure. (Everyone fails sometimes, it is a factor in life – just don't make one failure become more important than the many successes!)

These techniques will not guarantee success, and may even seem a little weird, but they are worth trying because they can increase the likelihood of success in future performance. Acting more confidently can make you more confident. Spend some time observing the behaviour of confident people and watch the reaction of others towards them. You may notice that people respond more positively towards confident people than to those who lack confidence. Start practising confident, positive thinking for yourself, listen to your self-talk and check that it is repeating the positive aspects of your performance rather than dwelling on the negative. The old saying 'nothing succeeds like success' has an element of truth, and if you act successfully you will become more successful.

Tutorial and peer support: mutual reassurance

There are many levels of support available to students – from personal tutors to academic support tutors and staff offering specialist advice on disability, financial matters or career prospects. Students are able to access all the support offered, although the majority may probably only access the academic support from course tutors on a regular basis.

Opportunities to discuss your work with the course tutor are usually built into the course structure. Tutors are there to advise you and support you in your learning. They do want to help, but also need to balance the support that you need as an individual against the needs of the whole group, so the length of each tutorial session may be limited. All students have a responsibility to manage their own study time, so consider how to use the tutorial support effectively – for example, by noting down the questions to which you need answers before you attend your allocated tutorial time slot.

Getting help from tutors on a regular basis enables you to focus your study in a way that benefits you as an individual. The constructive comments made and the action plans created should give added direction to your learning. However, during course sessions you will also gain support from fellow students, and can offer mutual support through discussion and the sharing of information. Other students may offer constructive comments on your work, and it is important to think of these as learning opportunities, not as implied criticism. By listening and sharing ideas collaboratively, rather than competitively, you may find that everyone benefits.

Setting priorities

As already discussed, the challenge of new learning, of being assessed on what you do and undertaking an additional workload associated with a course of study can lead to feelings of anxiety, which in turn inhibits learning. Plan to reduce some anxiety by setting long-term goals with short-term targets that keep the whole manageable. Allocate slots of time to complete the targets set – even if these are relatively short, you may find that by taking conscious control of what you do, you feel less anxious.

Here are a few reminders (in no particular order) of other things that you can do that may help to reduce anxiety. Some may seem fairly obvious, but it is sometimes the small, obvious things that get overlooked!

- Set your own priorities – you need balance in your life! Your family, your friends, your health and your work are all important, so do not neglect them as you start on a new course. Make time and do not feel guilty when you are with friends and family – instead, ensure that you stick to your timetable and give yourself credit for being able to enjoy all the different aspects of your life, for, as Covey asks 'How many people on their deathbed wish they'd spent more time at the office?' (Covey et al., 1994, p. 16).

- Take one step at a time – give yourself time to reflect, and try not to do everything at once. Learn from your mistakes, but do not feel guilty when you do make mistakes! *Trust* yourself! Have a go, and do not worry about getting things wrong. Remember that tutors are just people who have a job to do, and although that should command respect it also means that you have an expert to ask for help. Never feel that your questions are unimportant or that they make you look stupid – asking for help is the surest way of finding out how to do something!

- Use the resource opportunities that are available – share ideas and materials with other students. You are not in competition with each other – work as a team with a shared goal. Keep important details (assignment brief, Harvard referencing rules, timetables) readily to hand and refer to them often so that you do not make errors.
- Keep a timetable for your course: find out the dates and times for lectures/sessions and be on time, note the dates when assignments have to be handed in and the procedures for extensions. Plan any work-based activities that you may have to undertake and enter deadlines for these in your diary.
- Take notes during teaching sessions to help you afterwards – these should be brief but meaningful, such as mind maps, key words and phrases; do not spend so much time taking notes that you miss the point of the lecture! If for any reason you have to miss a session, ask a friend to take notes for you.
- Use the library, web resources, work colleagues and friends as support and as sounding boards for your ideas. Consider reading in short bursts of time and being critically reflective in that reading – read only what is relevant and necessary! Also, note the full reference for any book that you browse or read before you return the book to the library!
- Get used to the jargon! Whenever you come across a word that you do not recognise, either ask for the meaning or note the word and check up the meaning later. Try to use the words that you learn in your discussion and in your assignments; make new words part of your everyday language. Never be put off by a tutor using unfamiliar terms – look past the words to the meaning, or ask for an explanation.
- Use the support facilities that are available – there will be wide range of staff to help you, from the librarian to the computer expert, to those with specialist study skills to help you with constructing essays or staff offering financial advice. Ask for help when you need it – the tutor, your colleagues at work, other students, your family and friends – most people love the feeling of being needed and enjoy advising and helping others.
- Sometimes, creating a simple tick list may help you to be more confident. Try ticking off all the positive comments in the list opposite and remember to feel good about what you do know and can do, rather than always focusing on what you still have to learn! It may help if you create your own list with your own goals, and tick these off as you work through your course or programme of study.

Recording success

Tick any of the following statements that apply to you.

Course knowledge and learning		Personal study skills	
I plan work and leisure carefully and have created a timetable for myself.		I have the study characteristics of persistence, determination and hard work.	
I increasingly understand what is expected of me during study.		I believe that I am a learner and that I continually learn from others, from the environment and from personal study.	
I enjoy listening to others during discussion, and also like to take part.		I am supportive of fellow students, non-competitive and enjoy being part of a strong support network.	
I take notes during taught sessions and find these easy to follow afterwards.		I set goals for myself, and feel good when I notice that I am getting closer to achieving them.	
I am interested in my chosen study subjects and enjoy reading about them.		I do not panic when given assignments, but logically plan how to tackle the task.	
I proof-read my assignments and check spellings, grammar and structure.		I am a good time-keeper, and turn up for lectures and sessions on time with the appropriate materials.	
My first priority for assignments is to understand the requirements and use the information to study and write in a relevant and appropriate way.		I am pro-active in ensuring that I have all the relevant available information and do not hesitate to ask tutors for advice.	
When writing assignments I reference reading correctly and set out the bibliography in the accepted style.		I am steadily gaining confidence as a learner and know that I will successfully reach the end of my course of study.	

If you have ticked most of these, then you can feel satisfied with progress so far. You might like to reflect upon your success and consider how to improve further. If you do not feel successful, stop and list the reason for this. Which small steps would help you to become more successful?

Summary

As you read this last chapter, you may have realised that the general study guidance given in this book is not as intimidating as you first thought, and all of it is manageable once you know how. There may still be areas that you wish to revisit and, no doubt, improve upon as you progress. The aim of this book has been to reduce anxiety and to make higher education more accessible through understanding of the mechanics of academic study and expectations. A belief in your ability to succeed is perhaps the most important attitude to take with you into study. Hopefully, that belief has been confirmed and you feel more able to meet the demands that your chosen programme of study will ask of you.

Further reading

Students often ask the question, 'How many books should I use in my assignment?' and the answer is usually, 'How long is a piece of string?'! Not a very satisfactory answer, but it does indicate that you really cannot read too much. Each writer will offer a slightly different view, or even seem to contradict another writer in the same field. Generally, in academic study this offers an opportunity to demonstrate an understanding of the key issues and to give a balance of views in assignment writing and begin to reflect upon the themes. It also offers the opportunity to put forward a view of your own, agreeing or perhaps disagreeing with the writer's view.

You may not be required to write an essay on study techniques, but the principle given above is still applicable. Therefore, examples of texts for further reading for study are suggested below, including some from previous chapters, where authors' names and search terms have been given to help you to begin to locate your own study resources. The titles in this list may also provide a starting place for searching for similar titles in the library or online.

General study guides

Burns, T. (2012) *Essential study skills: the complete guide to success at university* (3rd edn). London: Sage.

Cottrell, S. (2008) *The study skills handbook, 3rd edition*. Basingstoke: Palgrave Study Guides.

Cottrell, S. (2012) *Study skills connected: using technology to support your studies*. Basingstoke: Palgrave Macmillan.

Drew, S. and Bingham, R. (2010) *The guide to learning and study skills: for higher education and at work*. Farnham: Gower.

Hargreaves, S. (2012) *Study skills for students with dyslexia*. Thousand Oaks, CA: Sage Publications.

Helyer, R. (2010) *The work-based learning student handbook*. Basingstoke: Palgrave Macmillan.

McMillan, K. (2012) *The study skills book*. Harlow: Pearson Education.
Wilson, E. (2009) *Effective study skills for part-time and distance learners*. New York: Pearson Prentice Hall.

Aspects of English: writing and grammar

The titles listed here offer basic advice for writing in an academic style.

Betteridge, A. (2011) *Chambers adult learner's guide to spelling*. London: Chambers Harrap Publishing Ltd.
Fairbairn, G. and Winch, C. (2011) *Reading, writing and reasoning: a guide for students, 3rd edition*. Buckingham: Open University.
Harrison, M. (2012) *Improve your grammar*. Basingstoke: Palgrave Macmillan.
Palmer, R. (2002) *Write in style: a guide to good English* (2nd edn). London: RoutledgeFalmer.
Peck, J. (2012) *The student's guide to writing: grammar, punctuation and spelling, 3rd edition*. Basingstoke: Palgrave Macmillan.
Rose, J. (2012) *The mature student's guide to writing, 3rd edition*. Basingstoke: Palgrave Macmillan.
Shields, M. (2010) *Essay writing: a student's guide*. London: Sage.
Wyse, D. (2012) *The good writing guide for education students, 3rd edition*. London: Sage.

Reflection, critical analysis, referencing and ways of working

Buzan, T. (2011) *Buzan's study skills: mind maps, memory techniques, speed reading*. Harlow: BBC Active.
Cottrell, S. (2011) *Critical thinking skills: developing effective analysis and argument, 2nd edition*. Basingstoke: Palgrave Macmillan.
Judge, B. (2009) *Critical thinking skills for education students*. Exeter: Learning Matters.
Neville, C. (2010) *The complete guide to referencing and avoiding plagiarism* (2nd edn). Maidenhead: Open University Press.
Pears, R. and Shields, G. (2010) *Cite them right: the essential referencing guide*. Basingstoke: Palgrave Macmillan.
Williams, K. (2012) *Reflective writing*. Basingstoke: Palgrave Macmillan.

Dissertations, exams and other types of assignments

Many of the books in the general study skills section will have chapters dealing with exam techniques and longer assignments. However, there are also a number of books written specifically with advice for writing longer assignments.

Bell, J. (2011) *Doing your research project: a guide for first-time researchers in education, health and social science, 5th edition*. Maidenhead: McGraw-Hill Open University Press.
Robert-Holmes, G. (2011) *Doing your early years research project: a step-by-step guide, 2nd edition*. London: Sage.
Simons, H. (2009) *Case study research in practice*. London: Sage.
Tracy, E. (2006) *The student's guide to exam success, 2nd edition*. Buckingham: Open University Press.
Van Emden, J. (2010) *Presentation skills for students*. Basingstoke: Palgrave Macmillan.

Reassurance, relaxation and fun!

Buzan, T. (2010) *The mind map book: unlock your creativity, boost your memory, change your life.* Harlow: BBC Active, Pearson Education Group.

Claxon, G. (2007) *The creative thinking plan: how to generate ideas and solve problems in your work and life, 2nd edition.* London: BBC Books.

Covey, S. R. (2005) *The 7 habits of highly effective people; personal workbook.* London: Simon and Schuster.

Covey, S. R., Merrill, A.R. and Merrill, R.R. (2012) *Summary: first things first* [Kindle edition], Must Read Summaries; Amazon Media EU S.à. r.l.

Johnson, S. (1998) *Who moved my cheese? An amazing way to deal with change in your work and in your life.* New York: Penguin Putnam Inc.

McDermott, S. (2007) *How to be a complete and utter failure in life, work and everything: 44 1/2 steps to lasting underachievement, 2nd edition.* Harlow: Pearson Education Limited.

Taylor, M. (n.d.) *Mind maps: quicker notes, better memory, and improved learning 2.0* [Kindle Edition]. Amazon Media EU S.à. r.l.

Websites

The internet can be a great place to start researching, but sometimes the material found cannot be counted on as being either accurate or reliable. However, many of the author names and themes in this book can be searched for further details, and this may be a starting place for a more focused search. Sometimes a website address contains clues as to whether or not it is likely to contain sound information. For example, look out for these letters in the website address (URL):

.ac.uk	Means 'academic' and indicates a university website.
.org	Used by large organisations, including research groups.
.gov.uk	UK government departments, including Department for Education.

The other factor to take into account when searching websites is that they may change content or even disappear overnight! Therefore, the websites listed below are offered as examples of what might be available. Remember to bookmark the sites that you are likely to want to revisit in your favourites/bookmarks folders so as to be able to find them again!

University websites

James Cook University, Australia: http://www-public.jcu.edu.au/learningskills/resources/lsonline/index.htm

Open University Skills for Study, UK: http://www.open.ac.uk/skillsforstudy/

Publishers also have study skill websites. Skills4Study (Palgrave) is one of the best and includes podcasts as well as printed resources: http://www.palgrave.com/skills4study/.

Organisation websites

MERLOT is a free resource designed primarily for faculties and students of HE. Links to online learning materials are collected here, along with annotations such as peer reviews and assignments: http://www.merlot.org/Home.po

NFER (National Foundation for Educational Research) also includes publications related to study, e.g. 'Education on the web: a tool kit to help you search effectively for information online', by Emily Houghton (2012): http://www.nfer.ac.uk/nfer/index.cfm

British Dyslexia Association: includes online tests for dyslexia and some advice for students entering HE: http://www.bdadyslexia.org.uk.

Index